TIPS FOR
YOUR PERSONAL
CYBERSECURITY

NICK SELBY AND HEATHER VESCENT

Rosen
YA
™
New York

This edition published in 2019 by:
The Rosen Publishing Group, Inc.
29 East 21st Street
New York, NY 10010

Cataloging-in-Publication Data

Names: Selby, Nick. | Vescent, Heather.
Title: Tips for your personal cybersecurity / Nick Selby and Heather Vescent.
Description: New York : Rosen YA, 2019. | Series: Cybersecurity survival strategies | Includes glossary and index.
Identifiers: ISBN 9781508186403 (library bound)
Subjects: LCSH: Computer security—Juvenile literature. | Computer networks—Security measures—
Juvenile literature. | Online social networks—Security measures—Juvenile literature. | Social media—
Security measures—Juvenile literature. | Privacy, Right of—Juvenile literature. | Computer crimes—
Prevention—Juvenile literature.
Classification: LCC QA76.9.A25 S453 2019 | DDC 005.8—dc23

Manufactured in the United States of America

CONTENTS

THIS BOOK IS ALREADY OUT OF DATE
(AND THAT'S OKAY)

Every day there seems to be a new story about cybercrime: millions of credit cards stolen, private celebrity photos leaked, foreign agents interfering at the highest levels of government. It's hard for even the best-informed reader to know how much of this is real versus scare-mongering clickbait, and how to react regardless. Sadly, many people either become so paralyzed by fear that they vacillate between different strategies for too long/ Conversely, some decide it's all too much and try to ignore the topic completely.

The thing is, each of us is utterly reliant on cybersecurity in ways both obvious and unexpected. As a police officer, I've brusquely knocked on the door of the suspect in a cyber case only to find a 78-year-old retiree, innocent of anything but a yen for some specialized, icky, but legal inappropriate films. Our man made a rookie mistake by going for the free icky-but-legal films, unaware of the first rule of the web: if you can't figure out how someone makes money on a site, you're the product. Criminals had planted malware in his naughty movies and were renting cyber scammers remote access to his computer, unbeknownst to him.

Some of the hacks we describe will be old news tomorrow. Some will take on new and more insidious forms. And something new will pop up every time you turn around. That's okay—this book gives you the tools you need to understand what your digital footprint looks like to criminals, advertisers, investigators, and governments, and how to figure out and fix your vulnerabilities even as the specific threats change.

We can't tell you everything that might happen to you—some of next week's threats are being cooked up right now in basements and labs from Missouri to Moldova. But we can tell you how to reduce your risks no matter what. Security experts like to talk about OPSEC (operational security). And OPSEC is OPSEC—today and forever. It's not about specific dangers, it's about a mind-set of preparedness.

Understanding your digital universe and the consequences of your actions will reduce the things that can make you a victim, without your having to miss out everything the internet has to offer. This book will help you better understand the kinds of threats out there, and give you the tools and perspective to protect yourself. The rest is up to you.

NICK SELBY

ALSO, THIS BOOK WILL FREAK YOU OUT
(AND THAT'S ALSO OKAY)

To put it simply, you're in danger. Your identity, your bank accounts, your kids, and even your government are vulnerable to attack from cyber criminals around the world. That should freak you out. But this book is much more than a collection scary stories (although it's that too). It's also a toolkit for protecting yourself and your data in an increasingly dangerous online world.

The digital age has given us a dazzling array of products and services at our fingertips, but also created new and often unexpected problems. Security technology will continue to get better—and criminals will keep finding new ways to get around that technology. That's where we come in.

How to get your head around security in the modern age? Most people want to know first and foremost how to avoid getting hacked. That's the wrong mindset. It's almost inevitable that you're going to be hacked at some point in your life online.

Start with the assumption that even the most secure technologies are vulnerable. There's an ongoing war between criminal hackers and security experts, and that's not going to change. The only way we can "win" is to assume everything will be hacked, and take precautions to secure what is important. If you expect this inevitable hacking of your security systems, you will be able to understand the risk factors and monitor your security on an ongoing basis. You'll know the places you are vulnerable and be able to take appropriate precautions.

How to know which are the appropriate precautions? That's easy. Read this book! Many of the vulnerabilities enumerated in this book can be dealt with relatively easily, once you have the know-how. You don't need to have the most secure system, just the best one for your needs. Not sure what those are? We'll help you figure that out.

In a sense, hackers are helping us–in their own way. Every time they break a system, we learn something new about its vulnerability, and how to make it more secure. I personally look forward to the new and exciting ways hackers will point out the limitations of each new technology. I just don't want them learning on you!

HEATHER VESCENT

Your bank account is suddenly, mysteriously overdrawn. Everyone in your address book gets a desperate email from you asking for money. You fail what should have been a routine background check. Your TV starts getting unusual error messages. What's going on? Cybercrime can, quite literally, hit you where you live—and it's getting more common all the time as our lives get more connected and hackers more sophisticated. The chapters that follow tell you what to do when Internet bad guys make it personal—stealing your identity or your money, invading your privacy, bullying your kids, or even threatening your life. We also highlight some unexpected vulnerabilities in your smart phone, your browsing habits, and your household appliances, as well how to keep your personal information safe and secure.

KEEP YOUR IDENTITY SAFE

IDENTITY THIEVES CAN BUY, SELL, OR CAPTURE YOUR IDENTITY AND USE THE INFORMATION TO GET MONEY AND SERVICES`—OR USE YOUR NAME, CREDIT RATING, OR INSURANCE TO TAKE OUT A LOAN OR GET FREE MEDICAL CARE.

There are myriad ways for the bad guys to get your information and use it for all sorts of nefarious purposes—mainly, stealing your money, although occasionally for other kinds of fraud or to cover their tracks when committing additional crimes. That's one of the big reasons identity theft can be so devastating. If a criminal steals your credit card information, your bank will likely refund you the money that was lost. If the same criminal impersonates you to run an illegal business, however, then your problems just got a whole lot worse . . . especially since many law enforcement folks aren't up on the latest types of cybercrime, so "that wasn't me" might not go over well.

How does it happen? We'll examine the many methods of identity theft in the pages that follow, and we'll also show you how you can protect yourself from being a victim or fight back if you already are. The methods of ID theft range from the seriously low tech (such as digging through your trash for unshredded financial documents or stealing those new credit cards that the bank sends you unexpectedly) to sophisticated database breaches and other hacks staged half the world away by large crime syndicates to fund cyberterrorism operations.

AMERICA'S FIRST IDENTITY FRAUD
Philip Hendrik Nering Bögel had some financial problems, and he was a creative thinker. So in 1793, when things got too hot for the Dutchman (who was wanted for embezzlement at the time), he did what any forward-thinking identity thief would do today: He hot-footed it out of the Netherlands, setting forth on this continent a new city, conceived in parsimony, and dedicated to the proposition that Bögel deserved better. Calling himself "Felipe Enrique Neri, Baron de Bastrop," Bögel started being awfully helpful to early Texas leaders Moses and Stephen F. Austin in obtaining land grants. After being named Texas land commissioner, Bögel came to settle a Texas city that he named after himself. Today, visitors to Bastrop, Texas, population 5,340, can celebrate how America's earliest successful ID fraud operation netted one guy a whole city.

MANY TYPES OF IDENTITY THEFT Criminals impersonate you online for a range of different reasons and in a variety of ways. For cyberstalkers (see Amanda Nickerson's story), the impersonation is usually part of a larger cyberbullying effort. But in most cases, the motivations are financial. Whether it's designed to get bank cards or bank loans in your name, obtain credit in your name, or impersonate you to use your existing credit, identity theft is usually a gateway cybercrime—an initial act, atop which lie other criminal schemes. So really, "identity theft" should be thought of as a family, or a category, of cybercrime.

Even though it's common for victims to be reimbursed by banks or credit card companies, the damage done by ID theft can affect you for years. Your credit score and history are the main ways that banks, car dealers, and other lenders determine the risk of extending you credit, and the black marks can be hard to erase.

A Taxing Scheme One of the fastest growing crimes in America is tax return fraud, which can net identity thieves thousands of dollars for each successful impersonation they make to the IRS. The criminals get hold of your Social Security number and personal information, and then create a tax return in your name that shows a modest overpayment on your part. The return is filed online using software, and within days, the IRS sends out a refund to "you"—at the address given by the thief. The refund is typically made using prepaid Visa cards, which can be easily exchanged for cash or property.

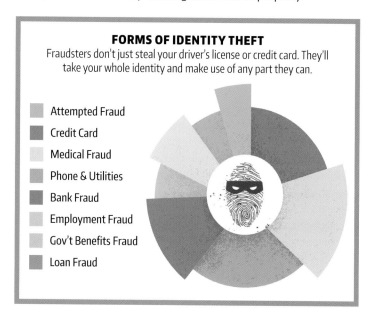

FORMS OF IDENTITY THEFT
Fraudsters don't just steal your driver's license or credit card. They'll take your whole identity and make use of any part they can.

- Attempted Fraud
- Credit Card
- Medical Fraud
- Phone & Utilities
- Bank Fraud
- Employment Fraud
- Gov't Benefits Fraud
- Loan Fraud

CASE STUDY

STRANGERS WITH CANDY In 2004, some InfoSec folks did a little experiment in which they offered passersby on the street a candy bar if they would tell them their work logins and passwords. To their surprise, some 70 percent were willing to part with the information—half of them did so even without the chocolatey bribe. You'd think that would have been a wake-up call. And indeed, governmental agencies and private-sector companies spend millions of dollars on training to make employees aware of proper security procedures and how important it is to follow them. How's that going? Well, when the experiment was repeated in London in 2008, there was no difference.

Whether the reasons are cultural or technical, the fact is, people are just really bad at keeping their passwords secret. They just don't take it seriously. What's even more galling to those who work with companies and individuals to improve security comprehension is that "your password" is still taken literally. By which I mean that most people to this day use just one password for many or all of their accounts—and a weak one, at that (see section on creating a secure password).

You might think that this problem would have already been solved with the creation of password manager apps, which significantly reduce the toil and trouble of thinking up (let alone remembering) strong new passwords, such as the ever-popular 98cLKd2rh29#@36kasgJ!. Plus, the programs are easy to use and can automatically change the passwords for all your online accounts.

So in 2016, when a security consultant decided to try the chocolate bar trick again, this time staging it as a contest in which the person with the "best" login and password would win prizes ranging from candy to a bottle of Champagne, he finally got different results: They were even worse than before.

SECURITY BASIC

GUARD THOSE DIGITS You should think thrice before handing over your Social Security number (or, outside the U.S., your national identity number), even if a legitimate office is requesting it from you. This number is a universal identifier, and you've probably been asked for it multiple times a year, every time you open a bank account, take out a loan, or verify your personal information. It always pays to think about why it would be needed and to refuse to provide it unless it is absolutely necessary. If you're paying cash, never give out the number. I would rather put down a $75 deposit to get electricity or phone service than provide the utility company with my Social Security number—plenty of utilities have been routinely hacked, and ID theft in America thrives on this ubiquitous identifier. If the service provider doesn't need it, don't provide it to them.

TINFOIL HATS It's a common joke that some people are so paranoid, they line their hats in tinfoil. Funny thing? That might not always be such a bad idea.

There are many ways to conduct data theft, and some of them do rely on secret transmissions. The best (or, at least, one of the coolest) examples of this was the Soviet hack against IBM Selectric II and III typewriters in the 1970s. About fifteen of these were used in the U.S. Embassy in Moscow and the consulate in Leningrad, and were modified by Soviet spies to contain a device that measured the magnetic disturbances generated when the little Selectric ball swiveled. Each letter, it turned out, had its own signature. By implanting a receiver in the walls (the buildings were, of course, built by Soviet contractors), the government could see the very pages of documents as they were typed up.

HOW THEY DO IT Criminals engage in obtaining identities to exploit in a range of ways, from low-tech to Secret Squirrel. Once the most common method of identity theft, paper or wallet theft is still popular, but now it's a small-time operation. Still, someone lifting your wallet and using your ID and credit cards can do a fair bit of damage. Similarly, ID theft can occur when people rifle through your trash and find bank statements and other bills with account numbers, balances, and dates. These specifics allow thieves to call those vendors and report your cards as lost, change your address, and have replacements mailed to them.

Other schemes to separate you from your identity run the gamut from physical theft of personal documents from service providers to breaking into a computer network specifically for the purpose of stealing data. Another popular method is phishing.

But of course, the most common method of stealing identities is to do so en masse in a large-scale breach of a retailer, bank, insurance provider, or government agency. This gives criminals the biggest bang for their buck and the largest number of targets. See the chart on the facing page for more information about how this works.

One Step Ahead of the Law It is very difficult for authorities to prevent or successfully prosecute identity thieves. Because much of the fraud can be done at a distance and by using online tools, catching the criminals in the act is difficult. What's more, with the global nature of the internet, the criminals don't even have to be in the United States to commit these crimes. And, finally, ID theft can go on for some time before a victim is even aware that it has happened.

HOW MIGHT YOU BE VULNERABLE? The vast multibillion-dollar cybercrime industry can be divided into three basic categories, each with its own objectives, although at the end of the day, the result is the same: You've been had. Understanding the differences, and what happens at each stage of the game, can help you stay safe. Here's how these crimes roll out.

IF YOU ARE

THE TARGET

THAT MEANS

an adversary has targeted you on a highly personalized basis.

IN THIS CASE, THE HACKER MIGHT WANT TO

extort money from your small online business.

SO HE OR SHE

crafts an email to you personally, using specific details to convince you he works for your website's registrar.

AND THEN

believing you're speaking to your own provider, you reveal the log-in information for your account.

ONCE THAT'S DONE

the hacker logs in, takes your site down, and changes your password.

AND IN THE END

the hacker demands a $5,000 USD wire transfer to restore your site.

IN THE TARGET POOL

THAT MEANS

you are part of a group being targeted by a broad-based or general attack.

IN THIS CASE, THE HACKER MIGHT WANT TO

access PayPal accounts.

SO HE OR SHE

buys or builds a spamming list of ten million email addresses, one of which is yours.

AND THEN

the hacker sends a fake but realistic and compelling phishing email that tricks you and other users into revealing PayPal account log-in information.

ONCE THAT'S DONE

the hacker harvests logins from anyone who fell for the phishing email.

AND IN THE END

the hacker logs into your account and sends himself a fraudulent payment.

THE VICTIM BUT NOT THE TARGET

THAT MEANS

you are a bystander caught up in someone else's mistake.

IN THIS CASE, THE HACKER MIGHT WANT TO

access health records at a major insurer.

SO HE OR SHE

registers a look-alike domain resembling the real one, say One-Health.com, instead of OneHealth.com.

AND THEN

the hacker crafts believable emails using a company executive's name, role, and title to convince users to open a malicious attachment.

ONCE THAT'S DONE

the hacker accesses the network, in this case gaining access to millions of private medical records.

AND IN THE END

your records are stolen even though you're not the one who clicked on the malware.

KEY CONCEPT

WHY IS IT CALLED PHISHING? Phishing is a term used to describe some of the most widespread and effective methods for obtaining information online. The term itself is a mash-up of two words—"fishing" and "phreak." The fishing part is just what you'd imagine: to fish for victims or data by using electronic bait, hooking victims, and reeling them in—an obvious and accurate metaphor for the act itself. The alternate spelling is a nod to the pre-internet practice of telephone-system hacking known as phone "phreaking," done by "phreaks." This is related to another hacker practice, called "1eet speak," which substitutes numbers for letters and some letters for others to create an often goofy insider jargon. It's quaint today, but you will still see versions in chat rooms, as hackers somewhat jokingly refer to one another as "133t H4x0r5," or "elite hackers."

TEACH A MAN TO PHISH Phishing isn't one specific thing. Rather, the term is used for a wide range of methods designed to gain access to your information. Understanding what those methods are, along with the basics of how they work, is central to both recognizing and avoiding many of the risks you face online. So before we go any further, let's do a quick overview of the many types of phish in the sea and the ways they can bite. Here are three common methods that these criminals will try when going after your data.

Voluntary Disclosure The first method is diabolically simple: Attackers use a rich mix of psychological techniques, known collectively as *social engineering*, to get you to give up the goods, essentially conning you into giving away the information that they want. People are generally trusting, and it's amazing how much information the average person will give up simply because someone happened to ask them in the right way.

Malicious Attachments In these cases, computer users are tricked by some compelling message into opening a poisoned email attachment, which then installs malicious malware on their machine, thus giving the hacker access to their computer or network. These masquerade as documents that the users "requested," photos they "just have to see to believe," and the like.

Malicious Links Because many email systems can now block out malicious email attachments, some attacks will use malicious links to drive the user to an infectious web page instead. Most people are so accustomed to clicking on links almost automatically that this technique is highly effective. Most of these links are disguised to boot—an image in the email with a logo or a line of text displaying an address or site to visit that is actually a cover for a malicious web address which a hacker has set up for just this purpose.

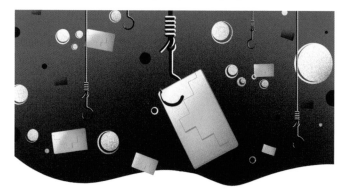

TYPES OF PHISH There are a lot of phishing schemes in the sea. You've probably been exposed to at least a couple of the examples listed below—and hopefully you didn't fall for them, although if you did, you're one of millions of people who have. Using the information below, you'll be better able to spot these scams and steer clear.

TYPE OF SCAM	HOW IT WORKS
CLASSIC PHISHING 	A fake website "spoofs" or closely resembles a real one, into which users enter their access credentials, identity data, or other sensitive information.
SPEARPHISHING	As the name would imply, this is a highly targeted attack, often designed to victimize a small, specific group or even one individual, using highly personalized messages that may be the result of hours or even weeks of online reconnaissance on the target.
WHALE PHISHING	The spearphishing of a high-profile or high-value individual, such as a CEO or celebrity, that is, a "big fish" or whale.
CATPHISHING	The use of fake online personas or profiles to create a phony emotional or romantic relationship, either for financial gain or access to sensitive information.
VISHING/SMISHING	Scams or data thefts that leverage phishing-like techniques but target phone users over voice lines or SMS.

IF YOU'RE ENTERING PERSONAL DATA ONLINE, TYPE THE ADDRESS YOURSELF AND CONFIRM THE SITE IS SECURED WITH AN HTTPS PREFIX AND A CLOSED-LOCK ICON.

PHISHING EMAILS ARE EASY TO DETECT

FALSE A lot of people believe that they can easily tell when they're being phished through email. But more and more often, scammers are crafting messages that appear to be from a legitimate source, such as your bank or your Amazon or eBay account, complete with a full page of images and icons from those sites duplicating a genuine email—but secretly redirecting an unsuspecting user to another site. You can sometimes confirm it's a fake by moving your mouse over the link (without clicking) and seeing another address pop up in preview. But just to be on the safe side, you should always enter the address yourself, never by clicking links.

- - - . . . - - -

DEFEND YOURSELF AGAINST PHISHING So if the thieves are smart, and not even the rich and famous can protect themselves, does that mean you're hosed? Not at all. That's because in most cases, victims fall for these attacks not out of a lack of resources but a lack of awareness. An astute and informed user with a zero-dollar budget is harder to victimize than an oblivious and untrained one with all the money in the world. Here are five simple steps you can take, starting right now, that will make you a significantly tougher target for phishers.

Be Aware Simple awareness is the first line of defense. Be suspicious. Understand and believe that you are a target. Treat any message in any electronic medium from someone you don't know as highly suspect.

Use the Hover Test Any modern email program will show you the destination of a hyperlink if you mouse over it without clicking. This "hover test" can help you spot suspicious links in any email you've received. If the visible link and the underlying destination don't match exactly, don't click!

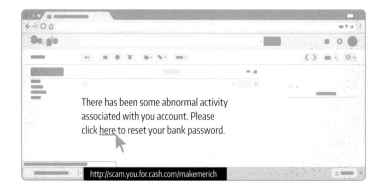

Check the URL Learn how to properly read a web address. The name of the site you're visiting is the last thing to the left of the first single slash, not the first thing to the right of the double slash. Phishers constantly use this lack of knowledge to trick people.

> **SAFE: https://www.amazon.com/**
> **UNSAFE: http://www.amazon.phishingforyou.com/**

Be Attachment Phobic Malicious attachments are the number one way to let password stealers, Trojan horse viruses, and other nasties get onto your computer. You should only open attachments from people you know, and even then limit yourself to messages you're expecting, such as an invoice for services you actually have received.

Confirm Out-of-Band If you happen to receive a suspicious message or a request for information that seems too personal, even from individuals or companies you trust, confirm the request via a different medium. For example, if they email you asking for your information or requesting that you click the link to their website to correct an issue, try visiting their website or calling them by phone. And remember, type the web address out manually or find the phone number yourself. Never rely on the link or phone number in the suspicious message. Those could both be fakes run by the phisher!

HACKER HISTORY

PHONING IT IN The first known online mention of the term "phishing" was in the online group alt.2600, a discussion forum for phone hackers, in early 1996. The "2600" refers to the frequency in hertz that early phone phreakers discovered they could play into a phone handset to take over the phone company's switches and make free calls to anywhere in the world. That this hack was so simple to execute, and so fundamental to the system that it was simply too expensive to fix, led to an entire subculture around building "blue boxes," or tone generators that would play the 2600 Hz whistle tone. Even Steve Jobs and Steve Wozniak, of Apple fame, sold them in the early days. One intrepid phreaker, John Draper, worked with some blind phreakers who were, as you'd imagine, particularly sensitive to tone. He learned that a plastic whistle offered as a free prize in boxes of Cap'n Crunch cereal blew at, yes, 2600 Hz. Draper used the whistle widely and became known in hacking circles as Crunchman. He's still around, too: You can find him on Twitter @jdcrunchman, or look for John "Captain Crunch" Draper on Facebook.

GOOD TO KNOW

YOU'RE NOT ALONE Millions of ordinary citizens have been victimized by one type of hack or another. Even the smart, powerful, and rich have been victims. For example, real-life rocket scientists at NASA have had their computers taken over by Chinese hackers. The U.S. government has concluded that Russians hacked the DNC and that Anonymous hacked Donald Trump during the 2016 election. In 2008, vice presidential candidate Sarah Palin's email was stolen by a hacker who figured out the Alaska governor's email password. Other notable victims have included Attorney General Eric Holder, FBI Director Robert Mueller, Jay Z and Beyoncé, Paris Hilton, Mel Gibson, Kim Kardashian—and Nick Selby, one of the authors of this book. This isn't even taking into account the massive amounts of top-secret government information released by WikiLeaks, Edward Snowden, and others.

KILLER APP

CAN I TALK TO YOUR MANAGER? The longest, most complex passwords are impossible for hackers to break in a lifetime (or even several!), but it also seems as if they might take a lifetime to come up with and nearly as long to input each time you have to use them. Luckily for you, there are password manager programs out there that can do all of the heavy lifting for you.

A password manager site or application like LastPass, Dashlane, or 1Password can generate, store, and encrypt a list of passwords for you, import any passwords that you have previously created yourself from browsers, analyze the strength of a password, and more.

Just be sure that you can remember and keep secure the master password to the account itself—and luckily, many password managers also offer two-factor authentication (see facing page) for an added layer of password protection.

CREATE A POWERFUL PASSWORD Now that you know what to avoid in emails, what's the next step? Well, every online account requires an account name (often derived from your own name or email address) and a password. The following guidelines can help you come up with passwords that are as unbreakable as possible.

One Size Does Not Fit All Look at the keys on a key ring: Each is a different design and cut. Just as each key is made to fit a specific lock, each password should be unique to the account it's used for. Otherwise, if you're a victim of ID theft, whoever stole your information will have access to every single account of yours that the criminal can think to try.

Bigger Is Better Some sites limit how long your password can be. While a long password may be hard to remember, it's harder for a hacker to break, even with brute-force methods (that is, using programs that try every single possible combination of characters).

Get Complicated Passphrases like "correcthorsebatterystaple" are easy to remember, but anything that uses dictionary words is easily hackable. Avoid simple substitutions, too, such as "p4ssw0rd" instead of "password." Use every single type of character you can: lowercase and capital letters, numbers, punctuation, and anything else available. Finding a number between 0 and 9 is easy for a hacker or ID thief; finding the right character in a total of sixty-two numbers and lowercase and capital letters is massively more challenging, especially the longer the string gets. If you have to write down a password to help remember it, keep said document hidden and safe from prying eyes or theft, or consider using a password manager.

Change Is Good Don't just come up with a password and then leave it be. Change your passwords frequently and, if at all possible, never reuse one. If hackers steal older data, they may score a hit if you're using that old password for a new account.

SECURITY BASIC

JUST DON'T The top ten most common—and thus worst—passwords have stayed largely the same since passwords became a thing, only changing in order from year to year. Right now the top contenders are:

1.	123456	6.	password
2.	123456789	7.	123123
3.	111111	8.	000000
4.	qwerty	9.	1234567
5.	12345678	10.	1234567890

WHO WANTS TO KNOW? Sometimes an extra layer of protection, called "knowledge-based authentication," or KBA, is added to your password, either in addition to your basic login and password or to verify your identity if you've forgotten your password. Of course, like many other defenses, this tool can also be turned against you.

Static KBA Also known as "shared secret questions," these are questions along the lines of your mother's maiden name, town where you were born, and so forth—often matters of public record. In addition, this information is stored somewhere, so it can be stolen, which means that even the weirder questions, like "Who's your favorite poet?" aren't secure.

Dynamic KBA Here, questions are generated in real time from a range of public and private records. You don't know what questions will be asked, but, hopefully, you'll remember the answer. Examples might include "What color was your Honda Accord?" or "Which of these streets have you never lived on?" You only have a short time to answer; the odds of someone guessing correctly on the fly are lower.

Unfortunately, you may not have the luxury of only patronizing sites with excellent dynamic KBA, although if you have the choice, take it. The simple workaround? Lie. It's relatively easy to figure out where someone went to high school. But if the "correct" answer is Narnia, Petticoat Junction, or Westeros, that's less likely to show up in old yearbooks. More's the pity.

SECURITY BASIC

USING THE POWER OF TWO Two-factor authentication, also called "2FA," is like a counterpassword in a spy novel ("The blackbird sings at midnight"; "But only under a full moon") or two people turning keys at the same time to launch a missile. Often available as a mobile app or a physical token (something like a key ring tag) that only you would have access to, 2FA uses a shared algorithm attached to your account. After typing in your password, you're prompted to use the app or push a button on the tag to generate the authentication key based on that algorithm, usually a short string of numbers randomly created on the spot. If an account offers 2FA (such as Google Authenticator), use it, and your accounts will be that much harder to compromise. If you should lose the token or the mobile device with the app, replace it ASAP so you can keep your account safe.

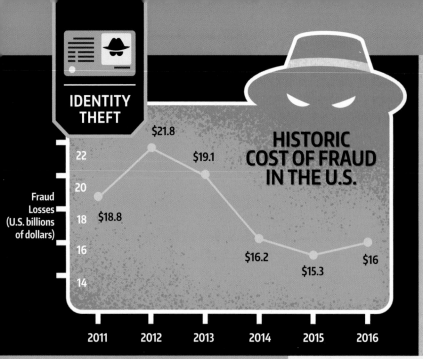

IDENTITY THEFT

HISTORIC COST OF FRAUD IN THE U.S.

Fraud Losses (U.S. billions of dollars)

- $18.8 (2011)
- $21.8 (2012)
- $19.1 (2013)
- $16.2 (2014)
- $15.3 (2015)
- $16 (2016)

22
20
18
16
14

2011 2012 2013 2014 2015 2016

90%
of victims report they weren't even aware that their personal data had been compromised before thieves tried to use it fraudulently.

64%
Credit cards that showed attempted or successful use by thieves.

30 HOURS
Average time to handle and settle a disputed charge with a credit company.

GROWTH IN CASES OF ID FRAUD

Millions of U.S. Fraud Victims

11.6	12.6	13.1	12.7	13.1	15.4
2011	2012	2013	2014	2015	2016

THE MOST TARGETED GROUPS

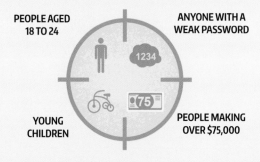

PEOPLE AGED 18 TO 24

ANYONE WITH A WEAK PASSWORD

YOUNG CHILDREN

PEOPLE MAKING OVER $75,000

COUNTRIES WITH HIGHEST INCIDENCE OF IDENTITY THEFT PER CAPITA

32%
of victims do not notify the police

1. MEXICO
2. THE USA
3. INDIA
4. THE UNITED ARAB EMIRATES
5. CHINA
6. THE UNITED KINGDOM
7. BRAZIL
8. AUSTRALIA
9. SINGAPORE
10. SOUTH AFRICA
11. CANADA

IF YOUR PERSONAL INFORMATION IS STOLEN, HOW LONG DOES IT TAKE TO RESOLVE?

48%	1 DAY OR LESS
16%	2 TO 7 DAYS
18%	8 DAYS TO A MONTH
6%	1 TO 3 MONTHS
3%	3 TO 6 MONTHS
9%	6 MONTHS OR MORE

SIGNS YOUR IDENTITY HAS BEEN STOLEN

YOUR CREDIT CARDS RATES GO UP

YOUR CREDIT RATING DROPS

MYSTERY BILLS SHOW UP

CAR INSURANCE GOES UP

BANK STATEMENTS STOP COMING

TAX REFUND DENIED

CAN'T RENEW DRIVERS LICENSE

CHECK-UP REMINDERS FOR MEDICAL CONDITIONS YOU DON'T HAVE

CALLS FROM COLLECTION AGENCIES

TURNED DOWN FOR LOAN

FAIL TO PASS BACKGROUND CHECK FOR JOB

30 DAYS
Average time needed to handle identity theft crime.

MOST COMMON FORMS OF IDENTITY THEFT

49.2%
ATTEMPT TO ACCESS GOVERNMENT DOCUMENTS*

15.8%
CREDIT CARD FRAUD

9.9%
PHONE OF UTILITIES FRAUD

5.9%
NON-CREDIT CARD BANK FRAUD

3.5%
LOAN FRAUD

3.3%
EMPLOYMENT-RELATED FRAUD

22.9%
MISC OTHER FORMS

*ID, social security number, tax returns, etc.

SECURITY BASICS

Your wallet often has all of your identification and bank cards (and more). If that wallet gets stolen, your entire life's identity and finances will literally be in someone else's hands. Should that happen, the best plan is to have culled its contents well beforehand so that you're only carrying the minimum number of IDs and credit cards—nothing more than is absolutely necessary. This will limit your losses in case of theft. And, it means that the only calls you will have to make will be to your credit card company, your local DMV office, and your employer to report the losses. Your credit card and driver's license will be replaced, and your employer can deactivate your work ID card, thus preventing whoever stole your wallet from using the card to break into your office and clean you out of paper clips and printer ink cartridges.

THE SEVEN-POINT ID THEFT RECOVERY PLAN If you have been the victim of identity theft, it is very important that you take steps to safeguard your good credit, warn the appropriate agencies of the event, and protect your good name. Often, you'll want to talk to the police. That's a good idea, but don't be surprised if you learn that there's not a lot they can do. The rest of this chapter explains how you can help yourself when you are the victim of identity theft. If you don't, it can cost you dearly when applying for a car loan, mortgage, or credit card. It could also make it harder for you to find a job, rent an apartment, or buy insurance.

The first thing you must do when you are a victim of identity theft is to get organized. The seven-step checklist here is just a suggested series of steps; customize it as necessary to your needs.

STEP 1	FILE A POLICE REPORT
	If you discover you have been victimized, contact the non-emergency number of your local police department and ask to speak to a detective.

STEP 2	GATHER DOCUMENTS AND EVIDENCE
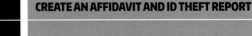	Contact your nation's consumer protection agencies, as well as stores and creditors to gain copies of the documents used to open accounts in your name.

STEP 3	CREATE AN AFFIDAVIT AND ID THEFT REPORT
	Your local consumer protection agency should be able to provide documents you will need and demonstrate how to present them. They also provide sample forms for an identity theft report, which, along with your police report, will help speed up the process with creditors, banks, and other agencies.

STEP 4	**INFORM THE CREDIT AGENCIES AND CREATE AN EXTENDED ALERT**
	To establish a fraud alert with the credit agencies, contact them directly. You will need to reissue the alert every ninety days.
STEP 5	**INFORM YOUR BANK, CREDITORS, AND MERCHANTS**
	With the package you've created, contact your bank and other creditors and merchants with whom you have accounts and inform them of the issues you have faced.
STEP 6	**PROTECT YOUR SOCIAL SECURITY NUMBER**
	If your number was misused, inform the national agency and request information on an ID Theft Affidavit. You may also wish to contact your agency if your Social Security number is being continually abused or phone to victims of identity theft.
STEP 7	**MONITOR YOUR CREDIT**
	You are entitled to at least one free credit report per year, but that is often insufficient for monitoring. There are several commercial companies offering these services, and we recommend you seek professional advice on which to choose. Several nonprofit organizations are out there to help victims, offering assistance to victims of identity theft by internet or phone.

SHRED AND THOROUGHLY DESTROY ANY OLD AND UNUSED CREDIT CARD APPLICATIONS OR SIMILAR FORMS TO HELP KEEP YOUR INFORMATION OUT OF THE HANDS OF ID THIEVES.

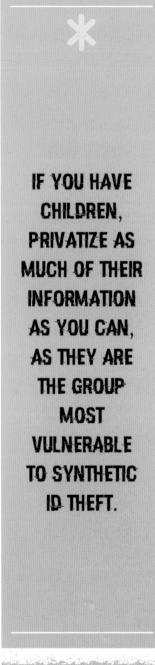

SYNTHETIC ID THEFT This chapter deals with the theft of someone's actual identity, but here's a new twist: synthetic identity theft. That's when an identity that has never before existed is created by scammers. Identity thieves typically seek to obtain names, national identity numbers and dates of birth, medical account numbers, addresses, birth certificates, death certificates, passport numbers, bank account or credit card numbers, passwords (like your mother's maiden name or children's or pet's names), telephone numbers, and even biometric data (such as fingerprints or iris scans). With synthetic ID theft, thieves only need some of this information to create a whole new fake person.

Thieves then create a credit file—the closest thing in the digital domain to conjuring up a human. This exploits a weakness in the authentication scheme used by credit reporting agencies: If an identity doesn't exist when it is checked, a new file is created. And a file? That's gold.

Credit Where No Credit Is Due The best thing to do with a synthetic ID is build its credit over time. This can be done in the traditional way—almost anyone can get a high-interest, low-limit, unsecured credit card at a hardware store, so the idea is to get one, then buy a hammer and pay it off over time. To get fancier about it, they might join up with a "data furnisher" who works at a business and will write up a phantom credit account for our spooky friend, showing scheduled payments made over time to speed things up. There's an entire industry around this, because the stakes are very high.

The most common way is to conjure up children. This is because, for the eighteen years or so after most kids are born, they don't do anything with their credit. During that time, anyone who establishes a credit file for the young one in question would likely be free from any interference until someone notices—that's typically at just about the worst time: when the kid applies for a college loan. The best way to protect against misuse of your child's credit is the same as it is for yours: Check it regularly, and check on it as often as you can. Should you happen to see fraudulent accounts, yell early, often, and loudly.

If you are on active duty in the military, it is recommended that you put an active duty alert on your own credit files by contacting any one of the three major credit agencies. Credit agencies all share active duty alerts. Each alert will stay in your files for at least twelve months. If someone applies for credit in your name, creditors will take extra precautions to make sure that the applicant is really you.

THE TAKEAWAY

Here's how to apply the lessons of this chapter, whether you're looking for basic safeguards, enhanced security, or super-spy measures to safeguard your privacy.

BASIC SECURITY
- Use strong passwords.
- Use different passwords for every site.
- Use a password vault program.
- Never share your login information with anyone.
- Don't click on suspicious links or download unexpected files.

ADVANCED MEASURES
- Always use two-factor authentication.
- Don't get kids social security cards unless necessary.
- Check your kids' credit at least quarterly.

TINFOIL-HAT BRIGADE
- If any service provider's site uses weak KBA, take your business elsewhere.
- File your taxes the old-fashioned way, on paper.
- Eschew electronic information wherever possible.

GOOD TO KNOW

WHAT LAWS PROTECT YOU? In virtually every place you care to look, identity theft is considered a federal crime. But it can still be next to impossible to actually get a federal office to investigate your individual case of identity theft—well, unless you are famous, or rich, or there is something larger at stake connected to the theft itself. Most states have their own laws against identity theft as well, and your local police department may have a program that can help you—ask them what resources are available in your area. Ultimately, however, you may simply be on your own, as it can be difficult to track down a specific perpetrator of identity theft (especially given that you may just be one of many victims caught in the same sweep). Usually, the best you can do at the local level is work to limit the damage done and clear your name.

WHERE THE MONEY IS

THERE IS MONEY IN CYBERCRIME. NOT "BUY A NEW CAR" MONEY. NOT "BUY A NEW HOUSE" MONEY. THIS IS "BUY A NEW AIRPLANE" MONEY, MAYBE EVEN "BUY AN ISLAND" MONEY. OF COURSE, IT'S MONEY THAT BELONGS TO YOU.

In his autobiography *Where the Money Was: The Memoirs of a Bank Robber*, America's most celebrated bank robber, Willie Sutton, denied ever saying that he robbed banks because "That's where the money is." Nonetheless, it's a great line. And for cybercriminals, it's a directive. Where is the money these days? On the internet. Even garden-variety spammers and botnet managers can expect to bring in $20,000, $30,000, even $50,000 USD a week. If you're bad at it, you'll make less. If you're good at it . . . well, the FBI said that the hacker and criminal-empire builder known as Dread Pirate Roberts was earning $1 million USD per week before his arrest. That's seven dollars and fourteen cents every second.

And you don't even have to be a criminal to pull down big bucks from hacking—even the so-called "white hat hackers" (also called "ethical" hackers) can have a payday, too. The FBI is said to have paid a cool million for the hack that enabled the bureau to access the iPhone belonging to one of the suspects in the 2015 San Bernardino mass shooting, and in September of 2016, *Wired* magazine reported that a high quality, previously unknown iPhone hack had been sold for $1.5 million USD.

In short, both bad guys and good guys hack . . . because that's where the money is.

SUCH A NICE BOY By all accounts, Maksym "Maksik" Yastremskiy is a nice boy. The twenty-five-year-old baby-faced Ukrainian was fun and friendly, and he bought nice things for his mother. He could afford to because in just about a year, young Maksik cleared some $11 million USD selling credit cards he and his friends stole from T.J.Maxx, an American retailer, before he was busted. Maksik's accomplice, Albert Gonzalez, was arrested as well. Perhaps suspicious of banks, Gonzalez had buried a barrel containing $1.1 million in cash in the backyard of his parents' home. Cops seized other fruits of Gonzalez's work, in the form of a new BMW, a condominium in Miami, his ex-girlfriend's Tiffany diamond, and three Rolex watches. So great were the stacks of cash he netted, Gonzalez bought himself the kind of currency counter used by bank tellers and casino cashiers.

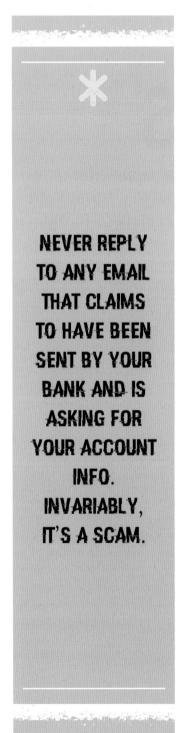

NEVER REPLY TO ANY EMAIL THAT CLAIMS TO HAVE BEEN SENT BY YOUR BANK AND IS ASKING FOR YOUR ACCOUNT INFO. INVARIABLY, IT'S A SCAM.

THE ELECTRONIC ECONOMY When the average person thinks of the economic side of cybercrime, what comes to mind is theft . . . someone stealing your credit cards or other funds electronically. And, indeed, this is a massive business, with some $15 billion USD stolen electronically every year. However, there are other sketchy ways that money changes hands (or flies out of your wallet) online. In this chapter, we'll examine a number of them—and how to protect yourself.

Identity Politics Often times, a phishing expedition or other sort of identity theft is just the first step in a series of attacks. While an identity thief may use data stolen from you for a number of purposes, as discussed in the previous chapter, the most common is to steal your money or use your identity as a shield for a larger theft. That's why it's so crucial to do your due diligence when you discover identity theft or fraud. After all, your credit card will almost certainly refund any fraudulent charges as long as you promptly report the card missing and file a police report, if required. However, if the thief then goes on and uses your identity to front a multimillion-dollar international con game, that would be a little less easy to resolve with a call to your local customer service rep.

Shady Sales Criminals don't have to steal your identity to get their hands on your money. You might be willing to hand it to them with a smile. We'll talk about the deep end of unofficial online markets elsewhere, but know that you don't have to be buying guns or drugs to be part of the underground economy. It can be much more mundane on the so-called gray market.

DATA THIEVERY

There are a multitude of ways that criminals can steal your data, from hacking into computers to pulling confidence scams.

- Viruses, malware, worms, trojans
- Criminal insider
- Theft of data-bearing devices
- SQL injection
- Phishing
- Web-based attacks
- Social engineering

NOT THAT KIND OF TRADING CARD As we were finishing writing this chapter, Nick's wife had data skimmed from her credit card. Since she checks her bank records regularly, she caught it the next day. The online history showed what are called "test swipes"—some $1 transactions, followed by a $49 test (many shops don't run authorizations or need a signature for purchases under $50), and soon after, a $599 purchase from Bed Bath & Beyond.

Her card data (the information in the magnetic stripe on the back of the credit card) had been grabbed by a fraudulent card reader. This data, known as a "dump," was gathered up with others into a pack and sold to a thief. This person downloaded the data and encoded it to another magnetic strip, such as the one on a hotel card key, which then would swipe just like the original card. Once we cancelled the card, the person using the stolen data dump breathed a sigh of regret, tossed the now-dead card on the floor, removed another from a stack of about a hundred they'd encoded from different numbers in the pack, and swiped again.

SECURITY BASIC

ELDER FRAUD A particularly cruel form of cyber theft targets the elderly. Every year, American senior citizens lose $2.9 billion to financial fraud. A study published by the National Health Institutes concluded that, basically, the older you get, the more susceptible you are to scams. Age was a stronger predictor than financial acumen, wealth, education, or health.

That's why so many online scams target the elderly. The over-seventy set is less likely to be computer savvy and thus falls prey to the "tech support phone call" scams, in which a helpful young man informs you that your computer has been malfunctioning; for just $29 USD, he can fix the problem. All he needs is a credit card number. This scam also manifests in a more aggressive form, as an "IRS auditor" calls to demand an immediate payment on mysterious back taxes. Wherever in the world you're located, you can find helpful tips on spotting and fighting common scams at the American Association of Retired Persons' website, updated monthly as new scams emerge.

FUN FACT

WHAT'S MY IDENTITY WORTH? In brief: not much, despite the damage fraud does to you. The aftermath of an identity theft can take around thirty hours' effort to repair, with losses averaging about $4,000 USD. But to an ID thief, you're just a drop in the bucket. A single dossier of a person's full financial and personal info might sell for about $1,300 to an interested buyer, but identity thieves often buy and sell in bulk. Files full of medical insurance info cost maybe a little more than $5 per stolen identity, while tens of thousands of Social Security numbers can be sold for as little as a penny per victim—so that list of 100,000 stolen SSNs (including yours?) goes up on the black market for just a grand.

KEY CONCEPT

FIFTY SHADES OF GRAY MARKET

Most of us have at least heard of black-market goods. But what about the gray market? Both gray- and black-market goods are purchased outside of the usual channels, compared to white-market (totally legit) merchandise. The difference is legality: Gray-market items may be technically legal, such as single items sold from a bulk pack or merchandise sent from a cheaper to more-costly region (such as from Scandinavia to the United States).

Gray becomes black, and thus totally illegal, when goods are faked or counterfeited. It's often hard to tell whether you're getting the real deal or if that "Viagra" contains an overdose of the drug or nothing but blue printer's ink and plaster. Some black-market items are even malicious or actively harmful and thus considered red-market.

WHAT ELSE IS ON SALE? A comprehensive list of all the merchandise in each market out there would take up volumes. But here are some examples of each (we'll get into the more serious stuff elsewhere).

 White Market: Taxed, licensed products and services; whatever you find on your local stores' shelves or on mainstream commercial sites like Amazon

 Gray Market: Untaxed legitimate products; taxed but unlicensed products; smuggled cigarettes or medicines, used merchandise resold as new; certain imported vehicles

 Black Market: Illegal unlicensed sales: counterfeit merchandise, stolen identities, drugs, weapons, fake IDs

 Red Market: Illegal offerings actively causing physical harm: murder-for-hire, arms trafficking, slavery, abuse

I KNOW A GUY WHO KNOWS A GUY That new game you wanted for your console this holiday season? It's now so in demand that it's on back order at the local department store, but your buddy knows a guy who works in the stockroom, and he knows when the next shipment is coming. What about that all-important textbook for your daughter's last college course? It's nearly worth its weight in gold at the university bookstore, but her roommate got a copy from Indonesia on eBay at a fraction of the cost! Maybe you need a new fridge, and you can't afford to shell out full price, but your friend says he can get you one, cheap—it just fell off the back of the truck when being unloaded is all . . .

These, in a nutshell, are gray-market goods: They're still legal, and you're still paying for them, but you're not exactly getting them through regular channels.

Just a Little Shady It's not quite a crime to possess or buy gray-market goods. Most goods for sale through these channels have been rerouted from different markets (so taxes may not have been paid on them), and trying to find them is sometimes sketchy, but they're the genuine article nonetheless.

Staying Safe Most gray-market merch is perfectly normal, but some shadier dealers will sell pre-owned items as brand new or offer defective merchandise without letting you know. If your "new" game console conks out on you, you're out some scratch and probably more than a bit frustrated—but if that scuffed-up box of "new" brake pads turns out not to give your brakes enough grip at the wrong time? *Caveat emptor* is the phrase that comes to mind.

GOOD TO KNOW

TOO GOOD TO BE TRUE The internet is full of knockoff and counterfeit goods. Here are some common examples.

Clothing and Fashion Accessories Because they are low tech and easy to make, brand-name fashions, watches, handbags, and other often-pricey accessories are massively counterfeited all over the world.

Footwear By some estimates, when you combine fashion and athletic shoes, brand-name footwear is the most counterfeited product category in the world, with fakes making up as much as one pair in ten worldwide.

Consumer Electronics A smartphone or PC might seem like a hard thing to copy, but it isn't for the thousands of firms that supply the same parts to the legitimate manufacturers.

Health and Beauty Products Gray-market sales of health and beauty aids run to 20 percent of authorized sales in most markets . . . and as high as 50 percent of authorized sales in some. That may seem harmless, but knockoff makeup and toiletries can cause severe allergic reactions, so shop accordingly.

T/F

TONER IS WORTH MORE THAN GOLD

TRUE Toner cartridges for your laser printer are ridiculously expensive, and most of what you're buying is the cheap plastic casing. The cost, and the value to the consumer, is in the few ounces of toner inside. Online fakes routinely sell for 10 to 20 percent of retail but could destroy your expensive printer. Don't risk it. Another example of these economic forces is that of cigarettes. Highly taxed, simple to produce, and high-value by weight, cigarettes are perfect for counterfeiting. Do counterfeiters take advantage of this? Well, consider that border authorities in the UK intercept an average of one million counterfeit cigarettes— every single day.

TAKING A GAMBLE So, what if you see an item that's almost certainly too good to be legit, but you're willing to turn a blind eye to the writing on the wall for a really, really good deal? From an ethics standpoint, you're on your own. We're not going to tell you it's ever okay to rip off the original manufacturers or sellers—after all, if everyone just photocopies this book and sells the copies on eBay, we'd be out of work. That said, here's the spectrum from "don't do it" to "really, really don't do it." The answer actually depends on what you're trying to avoid. Here's a good framework for how to think about making safe, informed purchases on the internet.

Rolling the Dice If you don't mind buying a cheap knockoff of designer fashions or accessories, you'll find a wealth of them online. Just understand that copies can range from totally worthless junk all the way up to identical goods made by contract suppliers on the same production line as the originals. If you understand the risks and feel like taking a chance, the worst you'll do is waste some money on a really obvious fake "Katey Spadde" handbag.

Watch for Counterfeits Some items are so prone to counterfeiting and knockoffs that, if you must buy online and want to ensure they're real, buy only from reputable sellers. Shoes from Zappos, toner from Staples, car parts from AutoZone, or CDs from Amazon are likely fine due to the strict controls used by these major retailers. The same goods from unknown sellers on eBay or Alibaba are almost certainly fake. That's okay for stockings, less so for your auto parts.

Never Ever Some things you should just never buy sight unseen online. This list includes significant assets, such as cars, boats, real estate, and so forth, which likely won't exist when you try to claim them; high-end jewelry; and prescription drugs or anything else your health or life might depend on.

GRAY-MARKET ELECTRONICS MAY SEEM LIKE A GREAT DEAL, AND THEY CAN BE, BUT THINK LONG AND HARD ABOUT HOW MUCH YOU'RE GIVING UP BY NOT GETTING THE WARRANTY, SERVICE AGREEMENTS, AND SO ON.

BIG SCAMS One astonishing blunder was made not too long ago by an English bank that decided to save money by encrypting just the "sensitive" parts of its database. So, instead of properly safeguarding it all, they only did the "account number" and "date of birth" fields and such.

And then thieves broke in through the bank's online banking application and sucked down the whole database. About three weeks later, customers began receiving letters on beautiful, cream-colored bank stationery, addressing them by name and referring to their account with that began with the numbers 271 (hint: all that bank's accounts did). "Dear customer," it read, "We value your business and want to make your online banking experience as good as it can be. Enclosed is a CD-ROM to help you! Just place the CD-ROM into your computer . . ." Of course, the CD-ROM was a combination of keylogger, fake-online-banking, and man-in-the-middle applications.

Another big-bucks scam relies on employees being scared of offending a top executive. Because bosses can't stop posting to social media, like, ever, scammers can track their movements through updates ("Just got to Shanghai, great meetings with ProX. Check out these offices!"). An employee then gets an email reading "Hey, Louise," I'm here in Shanghai and I just met with ProX Printing. Apparently, we didn't get their invoice three months ago and they are furious. Please send a wire transfer first thing this morning to . . ." The then boss provides a banking routing number and an account number. This scam is a highly effective spearphish, because it relies on so many things that seem like private data but are actually public. It works. Often. To prevent it, ensure that wire orders always—always!—follow the same verification process, by voice and with backups like second authorizers.

MOBILE BANKING As easy as it is to use your mobile phone to check your bank balance, pay bills, or transfer funds, you should still be wary, or even dispense with doing mobile banking entirely if you can. Aside from the obvious risk of losing your phone or having it stolen with any pertinent personal info on it (especially if you happen to have left it unlocked and unencrypted), there are two major issues with mobile banking: The apps offered by most banks do not support two-factor authentication, and furthermore, many of the apps will accept any sort of security encryption info—even false info that a hacker can use for a man-in-the-middle attack on the bank's security (wherein a hacker intercepts, alters, and relays information sent between you and your bank)—and thus the security of your own account as well.

HISTORIC HACK

YOUR GUILTY SECRET

One gambit that surfaces every so often is the story of the "hitman with a heart." It goes something like this:

"You don't know me, but I am writing to you because, even though I am a professional hitman with scores of kills to my name, I feel sorry for you. Don't even bother trying to trace this email or going to the police; it won't work. All you need to know is, someone who knows you wants you dead. I have been paid $5,000 to kill you. But you're such a good person, so I want to give you a chance. I was given $2,500 down, and I get another $2,500 after you have been 'taken care of'. But I'll make you a deal: If you pay me the $2,500, I will simply go away. I will not kill you."

You have to wonder: do these crazy schemes actually pay off? Given that they pop up over and over, they must pay off often enough that some people keep trying them, it would seem.

LOSING CONFIDENCE Historic confidence games, such as the Spanish Prisoner, were the inspiration for a deluge of emails that flooded the early internet. In the pre-internet days, this sort of con took some effort and time, and of all those envelopes mailed out by con men only a very small percentage found a gullible mark with money to spare. The internet changed everything—it turns out the only barrier was one of scale. Suddenly, hundreds of thousands, if not millions, of emails could be sent with very little effort or cost, and the 1 percent hit rate went from the occasional celebration to a sustainable business model.

The Nigerian Prince The most enterprising of these scammers were located in Nigeria. Spurred on by the internet, an exotic-sounding locale, and some early success, boiler room operations sprung up throughout that country, with dozens of employees acting as princes. The Nigerians became so synonymous with these kinds of scams that most people in the business still refer to them as "419 scams"—419 being the chapter of the Nigerian criminal code that bans fraud.

Stranded in London One modern scam takes advantage of how common global travel has become. The "Stranded in London" gambit begins with someone hacking into your email address book and harvesting all of your contacts. Each is then sent an urgent message saying that while on a trip to London you were arrested or mugged or injured and hospitalized. The story varies but always ends with a desperate plea for the recipient to wire money immediately. The same virus that steals the contacts also shuts down the email account, so you don't see the emails from concerned friends and family asking whether you're okay, how you got to London, and which hospital you're in. Versions of this are also used after takeovers of Facebook accounts.

The Spanish Prisoner On March 20, 1898, the *New York Times* warned Americans of a new scam: It appeared that a "robber and a humbug" was sending letters to Americans from Barcelona. The writer was in prison on political charges, but, thankfully, through hard work and thrift he had managed to squirrel away $130,000. Now, he wishes to enlist the help of an honest American, you (of whom he learned through a mutual friend of great character, whose name he will, out of an abundance of caution, not mention), to help spirit this sum to America so that his beautiful daughter can marry her true love. If only you would facilitate this transaction, a third of the sum is yours to compensate you for your time and difficulty. If you could, by placing in escrow a mere trifle—say, $100—to show your good faith, the transaction can proceed.

If this sounds familiar, it's because the Spanish Prisoner is the basis for the entire family of confidence swindles known as "advance-fee fraud." As you can see, this isn't exactly new—the *Times* article pointed out that the scam was—in 1898—already an old one.

THE TAKEAWAY

Make sure your money stays in your pocket (or your bank account or online wallet) by taking the measures below—at the very least you must apply the basics.

BASIC SECURITY
- Follow up on mystery bills or collection calls immediately.
- If you lose your wallet, report all cards missing immediately.
- If you get a text or email from your bank asking you for info, call a branch to make sure it's legit.
- If a get-rich-quick scheme seems too good to be true, it almost certainly is.

ADVANCED MEASURES
- Check your credit report regularly.
- File a police report after fraud of any amount.
- Only use CHIP-and-signature cards (or CHIP+PIN when available).

TINFOIL-HAT BRIGADE
- Don't use banking apps on your phone
- Don't shop online.
- If a store only has swipe machines, take your business elsewhere.

KEY CONCEPT

CONFIDENCE SCHEME
The idea behind every one of the scams you'll find within this chapter, from the historic to the modern, from the in-person grifter to the fictional Nigerian banker or prince halfway around the world, is the idea of the "con." These scammers are working to gain your trust in order to convince you to bring them into your confidence (hence the term) and to make you believe that their sob stories or their threats or their bribes are true. As the old saying goes: "If the story sounds too good to be true, it probably is."

Before you react right off the bat—whether you're doing so out of charity, fear, or a desire to get in on the riches—take a moment to pause, think it over, and spend a few minutes to do some research. More often than not, you'll discover that it's just another con and shouldn't be trusted.

PROTECT YOUR PRIVACY ONLINE

MORE AND MORE OF YOUR PRIVATE LIFE IS AVAILABLE ONLINE EACH DAY. YOUR WORK CONNECTIONS, YOUR SOCIAL MEDIA PROFILE, AND THE PHOTOS ON YOUR PHONE ARE IN THE CLOUD, MAKING YOUR LIFE AN OPEN BOOK TO CRIMINALS.

As high-speed internet connections become available around the world, more and more of our lives are migrating online. People keep their résumés on LinkedIn, tweet links to their Instagram feed, and use Facebook for pretty much everything. And those photos and videos that used to eat up your hard drive space? You stashed those online, right? After all, if everything is password protected, it must be secure! That's the promise of "the cloud," a fluffy name for a network of servers on the public internet that let you stash your private documents, photos, and more. Imagine a massive train station with multiple banks of lockers. Anyone can enter the station, but if you stash your valuables in a locker, only you have the key that can open it—until someone secretly duplicates your key (i.e., steals your password) or just pries it open with a crowbar (i.e., uses malicious code that compromises your private files).

The cloud is growing every day—and not just with private files. Massive companies such as Amazon, Microsoft, Google, and others are migrating from earthbound data centers into cloud systems, too. In other words, a lot of private data is going into a public space. If the last two chapters have taught you nothing else, it should be that this trend is like catnip for cybercriminals.

NOTHING TO HIDE One of my friends is fond of saying, "Unless you called the police, don't talk to the police." He happens to be a thirty-year veteran police commissioner who probably knows what he's talking about. Why is this relevant here? Because the idea that "I haven't done anything wrong, so I don't need to worry about being hacked" is about as naive as the thought that "maybe if I explain to the officer that those drugs weren't mine, he'll let me go." So, why should you lock down your Facebook profile when all you post is pictures of your cat? Because that open-book page is easily hijacked. The next thing you know, Mrs. Whiskerson is wanted by Interpol for money laundering. Or a hacker using your name and email is asking all of your friends for a $100 USD loan. Guard your social media and other online accounts as carefully as you would other information.

FROM RUSSIA, WITH SPAM So assuming that the Russians, in some form or another, hacked the 2016 election in the United States, how did they do it? The size and complexity of the scheme is still being discovered, but here's one piece of it. Democratic candidate Hilary Clinton's campaign website was likely attacked by a Russian-linked criminal group using a targeted spearphishing barrage designed to look like it came from the Clinton campaign. The campaign's email system was breached, and those emails went out to her supporters. A whole lot of people who received those bogus emails clicked on them without a second thought. Each click got the hackers more access and information until they were able to access the campaign runners' accounts. The breach damaged the Clinton campaign multiple times before election day.

THE TRUTH IS OUT THERE As an increasing amount of our data is stored online, and our everyday lives unfurl in public, personal privacy and reputation come under threat in a number of new ways. And that means you need to update your strategies for staying safe. In earlier chapters, we've talked about broad-spectrum operations that seek to steal as much data as possible in the hopes that something will prove useful. In character attacks, the intention is often more personal and targeted, with the goal of damaging a specific person or group's reputation. These antisocial urges are nothing new, but technology makes it much easier to act on them. Back in the old days, this wasn't as easy to do. Today's troublemakers have more tools at their disposal that work anonymously—but you can still protect yourself and fight back. First, let's look at how they find your secrets.

UP IN THE CLOUD What we call "the cloud" is really just a bunch of computers sitting in data centers around the world talking to each other through global networks. These days, folks at a new start-up are likely to spend less time thinking about how many servers they need and more on how many cloud-computing resources they can use instead. The cloud provider takes care of all the hardware, software, security, and physical assets through these data centers, and it also assumes much of the risk of owning lots of technology. By relying on such infrastructure giants as Microsoft Azure, Citrix, Oracle, Google, and others to provide the basic infrastructure, as well as tens of thousands of companies to handle all the details, that new business can start up faster and focus on what it does best, as opposed to managing expensive, space-hungry server farms. Sounds awesome, right?

SAFETY CONCERNS As more and more companies go completely cloud-based, new vulnerabilities arise. While cloud providers are very careful about protecting their own resources from being hacked and destroyed, they are less able to influence what happens once data shifts into areas controlled by their customers. So, for example, it would be extremely difficult to successfully attack Amazon and gain control of its servers. But once that data has been dispatched to, say, an individual user's Dropbox account, it gets a lot easier.

We don't believe for one second that Netflix, or Amazon Video, or Gmail, or Dropbox are inherently insecure. But they rely on users, and users make mistakes. In fact, most hacks begin when someone makes a mistake. Picture a real-life delivery system: No matter how well the U.S. Postal Service protects your deliveries, once the mail is in your mailbox, it's your responsibility. If it gets stolen, you can't blame the letter carrier.

Remember: Even though John Podesta's weak password (which was "Fluffy1," by the way) may have played a role in the spearphishing attack on the Clinton campaign's official email, the attack would never have succeeded without a whole bunch of people absentmindedly clicking on an unfamiliar link.

This chapter talks about how to avoid those mistakes, what can happen if you don't, and how to clean up any resulting mess.

ANATOMY OF A CLOUD What we loosely refer to as the cloud is an ever-evolving collection of hardware and software—the servers that make up the infrastructure and the platforms and applications that let end-users access it.

REMEMBER TO TURN ON PRIVATE OR INCOGNITO BROWSING TO KEEP SITES FROM STORING COOKIES ON YOUR COMPUTER AND COLLECTING INFORMATION ABOUT YOUR VISIT WITHOUT YOUR PERMISSION.

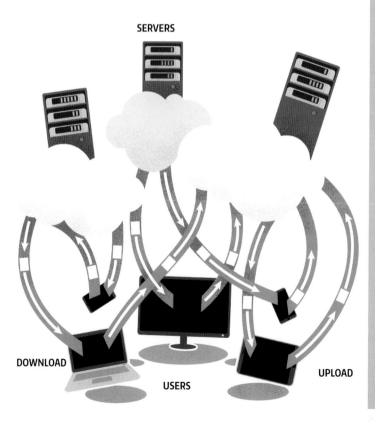

SERVERS

DOWNLOAD

UPLOAD

USERS

ONLINE ATTACKS, REAL-WORLD IMPACT

I'M A WOMAN WHO SPENT SEVENTEEN YEARS FIGHTING TO EARN MY TITLE OF VICE PRESIDENT IN THE OIL AND GAS INDUSTRY. IN A FEW SIMPLE KEYSTROKES, IT WAS ALL TAKEN AWAY FROM ME.

I used to think the internet was fun: posting updates about my life on Facebook, creating a LinkedIn profile to network professionally, tweeting random thoughts, and taking pictures of the world around me to put on Instagram—nothing prolific, just little things. Friends gave me advice about how online profiles could help my career in a future in which people would read about me online instead of talking to me in person. I trusted that the internet was a safe place to be.

Wow, how wrong I was!

I was thirty-seven years old when someone began to harass and cyberstalk me online. It began with false reports about me personally and professionally over numerous sites, from Twitter to Google+. The stalker created fake profiles of me on inappropriate sites, harassed me on social media, and threatened me over the phone.

Then the cyberstalker raised the stakes and began to attack my friends, my family, and my company. When I didn't comply with the demands made of me,

my tormentor posted bogus rip-off reports and reviews of the company I worked so hard to build. Every part of my life was targeted.

Until this began, I had never really understood the power of the internet or given very much thought on how I could navigate it safely.

As the cyberstalking intensified, as more information about me was posted in more places, I felt increasingly alone and that the rest of the world doubted me before even meeting me. I would walk into business meetings and be asked right away about intimate things no one would mention in the company of their own children, but because it was online, it was considered fair game.

People believe what they read online. Despite my efforts to set the record straight, I ended up losing contracts and ultimately my job. I couldn't trust anyone around me. I was under attack on all fronts. Some even exploited the situation to pressure me for money, blaming me for the impact my stalker had on their lives.

"FOR THEM, IT WAS A SICK GAME; FOR ME, IT WAS REALITY."

Two years of relentless psychological terrorism left me feeling hopeless, helpless, and powerless. I had been completely violated. I had nowhere to turn, since all of my attempts to involve the FBI and local police were met with the same answer: "We don't have the resources to help with a situation that doesn't involve murder." All I wanted was the answer to a simple question: "Why me?" Why would a stranger have so much hatred and feel the need to destroy a hardworking woman?

My now-husband and I had just started dating, and so it seemed likely that the attacks started out as an attempt by some unknown person to break us up. Instead, it forged us in fire. We were both broken to our cores, but we found our true love. We were married in the middle of this merciless attack, and now I have a teammate who is at my side until the end.

Two years on, the attacks still continue. I was advised that if I keep a low profile the attacker would eventually lose interest, but so far that has not been the case. So this year, I decided that I'd had enough. I decided to create a blog outlining all that had happened to me and the tools I found useful.

I am making sure my voice is heard. There are very few places to turn, and many are scams that cannot help you. My personal blog, www.stalkerexposed.com, explores in-depth the harsh realities of what can happen when someone wants to hurt you online. It is meant to serve as a reminder to everyone to take action and be safe online.
—Amanda Nickerson

LESSON LEARNED

Amanda Nickerson believes that the best protection online is to have a good password and two-factor authentication on every site you can. As a proactive measure, bolster your legitimate online presence and keep it up to date. This is huge: The less there is online about you, the easier it is for trolls and stalkers to make your life difficult. Laws lag far behind modern tech, and many of the companies that host mean and outright made-up content on blogs don't even respond to complaints or demands. You'll end up having to hire lawyers to do takedowns.

Spend your energy on genuine and meaningful content about what you truly do instead of sinking time into fighting lies. Google rewards solid content with better rankings. It takes time, but your peace of mind and career will benefit from a concerted effort to curate a solid body of online content about yourself and your interests.

CHECK YOURSELF You might not be able to stop someone from spreading fake stories about you, but you can make the harasser less likely to be taken seriously or even seen in search results.

Start by seeing what your online presence looks like right now. Using Chrome, open an incognito window or use duckduckgo.com and search for your name within double quotes ("Nick Selby"). The results will give you a sense of what a stranger Googling you would see. How does it look? Would you hire this person? Sell this individual a house? Go on a date with them?

Every month, check again to see what pops up. If your first check reveals nothing unusual, this exercise is just a formality. If, however, you discover that someone is trying to make you look bad, step up efforts to generate accurate content. Over time, the real you should rise in the rankings, while illegitimate sites fall away.

WATCH OUT FOR TROLLS Unfortunately, there's no shortage of women on the internet who still have to face random and sometimes extremely vicious harassment for little or no discernible reason or cause. While we fervently hope that in a few years our admonitions will seem as quaint and antiquated as a warning about spotting a dishonest footman, right now we'd be remiss not to touch on this unsavory topic. Women working in traditionally male-centric fields, such as gaming or technology, probably face the largest amount of abuse, but trolls can sometimes fixate on the strangest of things. One freelance journalist was testing blogging tools in order to set up a site; she posted a single goofy article on why she loves broccoli before abandoning the blog. Yet even this one article somehow touched a nerve: An unhinged stalker found that single post and made her life hell for more than a year. He made assault and death threats (the standard currency of the sexist troll), PhotoShopped her head onto inappropriate images and mailed them to her employers and family, doxxed her, and even showed up outside her apartment to intimidate her in person. The threats never rose to a level that could get law enforcement involved, and it took her years to undo the damage. She still writes under a pseudonym and is very cautious about using any social media. Sound like a one-in-a-million crazy story? Not if you read Amanda Nickerson's case. In an even more unnerving case, best-selling writer Jessica Valenti recently dropped off all social media after the commenters who regularly threatened her with assault and murder started making the very same threats against the writer's five-year-old daughter.

WHY THEY DO IT Popular writer Lindy West was plagued by a troll who got under her skin by creating a Twitter account in the persona of her recently deceased father to pepper her with insults and threats in his name. She wrote a fascinating piece about how painful this was—and unexpectedly got an email from the man behind the account. The resulting conversation (which you can hear on the popular podcast This American Life) was both illuminating and ultimately frustrating. He said that when he started harassing her, he was filled with self-loathing and was infuriated that she, a self-described fat woman, could be happy and successful. Why did this inspire him to torment and harass her? He had no good answer for West. He said it just seemed like the thing to do.

DON'T BE DISCOURAGED So, what's the takeaway for the average reader? Despite all of the above, the odds of this kind of random, sustained harassment are low. And, counterintuitively, while raising your profile may attract trolls, it will also give the kind of robust, impressive online presence that makes it more difficult for them to harm you. If you are harassed, report and block as necessary, and don't let them scare you away.

REPUTATION MATTERS Modern commerce means doing business with all kinds of people you've never met but whom you still need to be able to trust. That's where online reputation comes in. Just as you have a reputation in your community, your school, your family, and with your friends, you also have one online that is based on your browsing history and activities.

The concept of online reputation was pioneered by the auction site eBay. As a global marketplace connecting buyers and sellers, the company had to offer tools to assure users that the strangers they are buying from are trustworthy.

If you, like so many people, use eBay, your reputation is based on whether you communicate well, pay on time, and send what was ordered . . . or whether you tend to stiff buyers or raise hell over trivial matters. On Uber, your ratings are those assigned to you by drivers after each ride. Airbnb users rate your home online, and you, in turn, rate their performance as guests. Right now, reputation is not transferrable—eBay users don't have access to your Amazon rankings, and Uber drivers can't see what Lyft thinks of you—but that might well change in the future as the concept develops. Reputation is perhaps even more important to small businesses.

SECURITY BASIC

EYES AND EARS In a 2016 photograph depicting Facebook CEO Mark Zuckerberg sitting at a desk, security folks noted that there was a piece of masking tape over the camera of his laptop. To those who wonder whether Zuck was being a little paranoid, he wasn't. In fact, closer examination showed that he had also disabled the microphone.

It was back in 2007 when I saw the first demonstration of a remote hack that stealthily turned on a user's camera and microphone, made a video, and sent it someplace, all without alerting the user. And the technology has really advanced since then.

To be safe, cover web-enabled cameras and microphones with masking or duct tape until you want to use them. This is what security nerds call a *positive security model*— that is, "deny by default, and allow by exception."

WARDRIVING IS THE "SPORT" OF SCANNING FOR UNSECURED, EASILY HACKED HOME NETWORKS. TO PROTECT YOURS, CHANGE THE DEFAULT PASSWORDS AND NAMES, AND ENCRYPT ALL TRAFFIC ON YOUR NETWORK.

SNATCHING SECRETS FROM THE AIR Hackers love Wi-Fi, because these networks form one of the weakest points in an average user's online activity. And once they've breached your Wi-Fi, they can do a lot more than download Netflix on your bandwidth. A hacker can track and hijack the data you send and receive and use your connection to commit any number of crimes that could then be traced back to you. I've been on cases where the police literally kicked down a door, guns at the ready, to bust a major child illegal operation . . . only to find a very scared and confused older couple whose system had been hijacked. In that case, they were lucky the responding officers knew enough about cybercrime to suss out the situation. Not everyone is so lucky. Read on to learn some of the most common risks you face when going online wirelessly and how to defeat them.

At Home Loads of home networks are completely unsecured, which means they don't require a password for access. This exposes everything you transmit over that Wi-Fi connection to potential interception, and if that sounds like spy stuff, it shouldn't. You can learn how to harvest this bounty of information, if you are so inclined, with free software and instructional YouTube videos. Some networks are password protected, but the typical home user usually retains the default password that came with their wireless router. If this describes you, you may not be shocked to learn that there are entire websites dedicated to cataloging the default passwords for nearly every router ever made. Secure your home network with a strong password and change it often to increase security.

In Public Hackers love coffee shops and hotel lobbies. Harried travelers and groggy commuters constantly use free public Wi-Fi connections with no thought for safety. If the networks are unsecured, they can be "sniffed" just like your home network. If they are secured, hackers may set up a second network that isn't with a deceptive name. For example, search for Wi-Fi on your phone the next time you're sitting in the lobby of a large hotel. You may well see a long list—some of them belonging to nearby residences or businesses. But in addition to the official Whitby Arms Inn, there may be networks named things like "Guest Rooms," "Hotel Network," or "Lobby Internet." They may even be cleverly named to be listed alphabetically above the real network and therefore easy to select. Always ask for the name of the business's official network, and if you have the choice of a password-protected option, take it. It might even be worth paying a modest usage fee for enhanced security.

SURE SIGNS YOU'VE BEEN HACKED Despite your best efforts at keeping your network locked down, there's always a chance that a black-hat hacker has broken into it. Luckily, there are plenty of ways to tell if that's happened. Here's a list of potential symptoms to diagnose a compromised network. (There are plenty of other possibilities out there, too; if something just doesn't feel right about your network, dig deeper and you might find something as the result of a hack.)

Missed Connections If your network is running slowly during an apparent quiet time, it could be the result of someone else using your bandwidth. Too many connections from too many users can clog a network, especially a smaller one. Check and see who's logged on, and make sure the devices belong to people you know and trust.

A Lack of Control Are you unable to log on to the network? That may indicate that the login or password has been changed; a sure sign someone else has gotten in and locked you out. Be sure you change your network's default password at the very least.

Taking a Drive If your machine's hard drive is running slower than usual, and you notice the activity light flashing a lot more than it should, look into the situation a little further: Your antivirus software could be running a scan—or someone could have broken in and used malware to scan your disk looking for interesting data to steal.

Shields Down Is your antivirus software disabled even though you swear it was set to start every time your machine boots up? Or even though you swear you just restarted it five minutes ago? A malware infection can often disable antivirus software.

Unexpected Wares Your browser window didn't have that toolbar the last time you used it. And those pop-up windows weren't authorized either. What program just started during bootup? You didn't set that up, did you? Check to see if any extra software has been installed that you didn't put in yourself. Chances are it's the result of a hack.

No Shutdown The system won't shut down when you tell it to? You could be prevented from doing so by a hacker who wants to stay on the system. (But you can always pull the plug.)

WI-FI HACKING IS SO EASY, A KID CAN DO IT

TRUE You don't have to be trained in information technology work, or even be an adult, to know how to break in to someone else's system. All you really need is a computer with internet capability and a surprisingly short amount of time.

This was aptly proven during an ethical hacking demo in London in 2015, when seven-year-old Betsy Davies was shown a free YouTube video tutorial on how to fake a public Wi-Fi hot spot, then used it to get access to volunteers' computers—and in no more than eleven minutes.

In short, anyone could be a hacker—even a kid on a laptop in a nearby library or coffee shop. And a skilled hacker with the means and the intent can do a lot more damage than a curious kid.

A TANGLED WEB OF CONNECTIONS

I'M AN INVESTIGATOR WHO HAS SPENT MORE THAN A DECADE FIGHTING CYBERCRIME. IT'S COMMON FOR CRIMINALS AND CON MEN TO CONSTRUCT FAKE IDENTITIES AND COZY UP TO PERSONS OF INTEREST ONLINE. OF COURSE, THESE TECHNIQUES MIGHT ALSO BE USED BY COPS. HERE'S HOW A TYPICAL ONLINE "FRIEND" IS CONSTRUCTED.

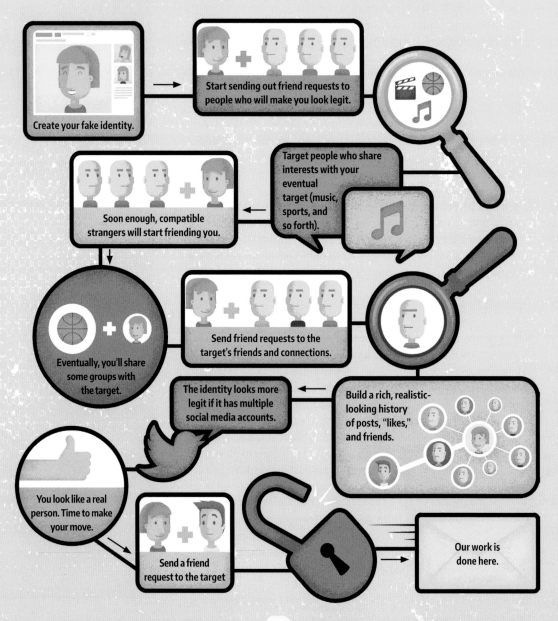

THE PROBLEM OF OVERSHARING Lots of parents think their kids share too much info online, and they're right; we'll talk more about that in the next chapter. But while adults may be less likely to suffer physical harm, bullying, or ridicule than their offspring, they're often just as guilty of sharing too much with their friends on social media—and the personal, financial, and career consequences can be significant. Consider just a few cases of grown-ups not practicing what they (hopefully) preach.

Watch Me Fly The CEO of a major gaming company spoke publicly about battling a series of hacks from an adversary called Lizard Squad. Sometime later, he posted online about a trip he was about to take. The hackers identified the specific flight he would be on and forced it to divert by tweeting a bomb threat to the airline. If the executive hadn't provided sufficient data for the hackers to figure out his travel details, his business trip wouldn't have been disrupted.

Expensive Tweets Michael Dell, the tech executive, pays millions of dollars a year for security to protect his family from potential kidnappers and other dangers. Finding that his teenage daughter had tweeted links to photos of a family trip, with details on where they'd be for the next few weeks, was probably a little frustrating. As evidenced by the swift disappearance of her Twitter account.

Feeling Indiscreet The Israeli army was forced to cancel a military operation after one of the soldiers taking part in it posted the location and date of their planned attack on Facebook.

Busted! A decorated member of the UK's Buckingham Palace Guard was sacked after ranting on Facebook, calling Kate Middleton, the Duchess of Cambridge, a variety of inappropriate names. Back in the more mundane world, internet meme sites are filled with screengrabs of Facebook sequences like this:

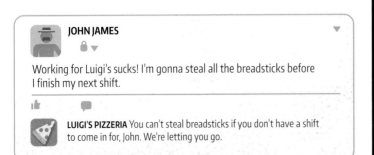

> **JOHN JAMES**
> 🔒 ▾
>
> Working for Luigi's sucks! I'm gonna steal all the breadsticks before I finish my next shift.
>
> 👍 💬
>
> **LUIGI'S PIZZERIA** You can't steal breadsticks if you don't have a shift to come in for, John. We're letting you go.

KEY CONCEPT

BUGS IN THE HUMAN HARDWARE Security consultant and former hacker Kevin Mitnick has said that it's often far easier to talk someone into giving you their password than to try to break into a system yourself. That's where social engineering comes into the picture.

While not necessarily a con in and of itself, social engineering can be part of a con scheme (which we already covered in detail in the previous chapter). Either way, it involves manipulating a person into giving up sensitive information or performing actions that allow the "engineer" to acquire the information: an account login, email, password, credit card, or other sensitive material.

Remember that most businesses do not ask clients for their personal information, and most social engineering attempts are never even made in person. It comes down to trust . . . so, do you trust who's emailing you or calling you?

DRAWING UNWANTED ATTENTION In 2011, our friend Aaron Barr, a man with years of intelligence and security experience, was a senior executive of HBGary Federal, selling advanced threat analytics and information tools to the government. Encouraged to put himself "out there" at conferences and in the press, Barr made a critical misstep: He said publicly that he had already identified many in the internet hacking community known as Anonymous. The result involved a social engineering attack against HBGary's computers that succeeded in breaching the email account of the firm's president and disseminating all the company's work and private communications to the public.

"I immediately wanted to fight to set the record straight," Aaron said. "I would even point journalists to specific leaked emails when they got their story wrong. More than one journalist said that he didn't have time to thoroughly research every story. In many cases, they go with whatever is hot and just get out what they can in the time they have."

Barr's side of the business went bust over the hubbub. The more he spoke out, the more dangerous it got—there were threats against his life and the lives of his loved ones. He and his family had to move multiple times. Ultimately, after a period of a few years of lying low and reestablishing himself, Aaron Barr has relocated, and he has begun to work again in an area in which he is particularly gifted: finding people on the internet.

Aaron believes that he should have laid low earlier and said less to stoke the flames. "I'm not the kind of guy to back down from a fight," he says, "but in this case, there were too many people, with too many motives to make me look bad. Shutting up and lying low was the best thing I could have done."

Tempting as it may be to share information online, stop and think at least once before you hit "post." Probably twice. Ask yourself, would it be safer to keep this closer to my vest? Am I likely to end up as the target of internet pranksters who may have no other goal than to prove themselves smarter than me (in their own mind, at least)? Would a major revelation help to fight cybercrime or just drive them further underground, spoiling for a fight? There are no one-size-fits-all answers, but you should take the time to ask the questions.

THE TAKEAWAY

Here's how to apply the lessons of this chapter, whether you're looking for basic safeguards, enhanced security, or super-spy measures to safeguard your privacy.

BASIC SECURITY

- Set all social media privacy settings as high as possible.
- Password-protect home Wi-Fi and encrypt with WPA2—never WEP.
- Don't accept friend requests from strangers you have not met personally.

ADVANCED MEASURES

- Only use the internet in incognito mode.
- Google yourself regularly and check what's said.
- Never use public Wi-Fi without a VPN.
- Restrict what you share on social media.

TINFOIL-HAT BRIGADE

- Keep nothing unencrypted in the cloud.
- Cover all computer webcams and microphones with electrical tape.
- Change user names frequently.

SECURITY BASIC

IS IT SAFE? Cloud storage gives us the promise that we can safely securely store any data we wish, and retrieve it at will thereafter—especially useful for small business owners. But the cloud is still ultimately a series of storage drives as part of a server in a location far away from your own—which means that any data stored there is likewise at a distance. If you lose connection with that cloud storage, or if the server goes down due to a hack or power outage, or if your account is compromised, you also lose access to all that data you've stored.

Basic data files, like simple documents, are mostly safe. But think twice about storing anything sensitive in the cloud, such as personal identification info, tax documents, or intimate photos and videos. Only store something if you're comfortable risking losing access to it or having it published somewhere online.

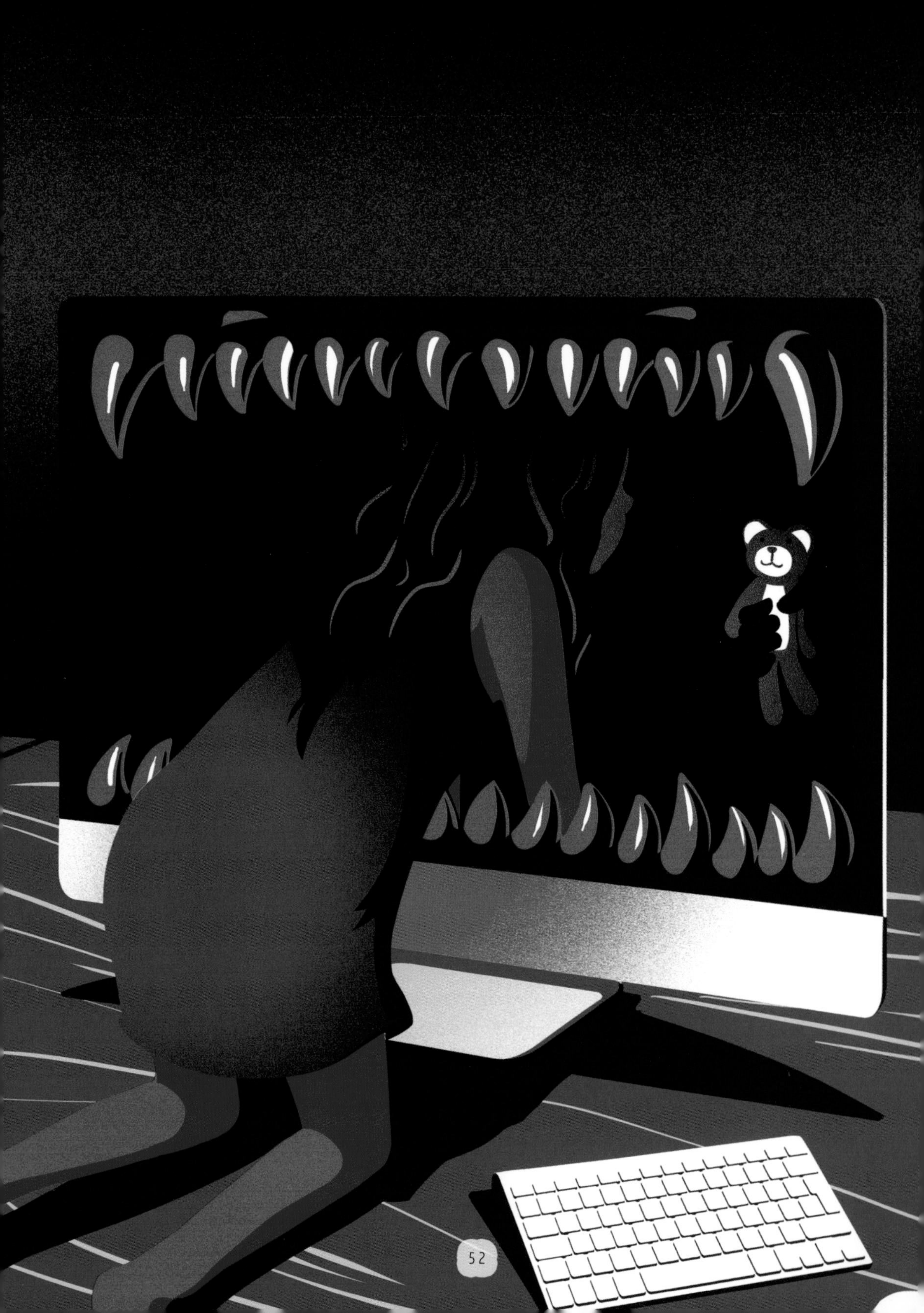

KEEP KIDS SAFE ONLINE

ONE OF THE BIGGEST CONCERNS PARENTS HAVE IS HOW TO KEEP THEIR KIDS SAFE FROM ONLINE PREDATORS, CYBERBULLIES, AND OTHER CREEPS. SAVVY PARENTS ALSO KNOW THEY SHOULD BE KEEPING THEIR COMPUTERS SAFE FROM THE KIDS.

Ask parents the fastest way to make their kid's eyes roll is and they'll tell you it's making the kid watch Mom or Dad interacting with technology. The generation of parents who grew up without smartphones, iPads, or the internet lack credibility with their children when trying to warn them about online dangers. If Mom can't figure out iMessage, how could she possibly know anything about internet safety?

This matters, because there are real dangers out there that your kids will almost certainly be exposed to—from online predators to annoying viruses that can destroy your data or encrypt your photos until you pay a ransom. Not to mention your kid clicking a video link that results in a spam gang using your router for distributed denial-of-service attacks against Walmart.

Kids born after the internet—sometimes known by us oldies as "digital natives"—grew up with this stuff and think nothing of digging into system preferences and settings we might not even know about. Which, in turn, means they can probably circumvent little inconveniences like that parental control software you installed.

The good news is that protecting a kid online has almost nothing to do with software and everything to do with straight talk.

IT ONLY TAKES TWO CLICKS In a New Zealand study on internet safety, researchers gave children between the ages of one and fourteen free access to a computer with unprotected internet access and told them to look for whatever they wanted online. Those kids ended up exposing the computer they were using to a virus within their first two clicks. No matter which topic they searched for, those two clicks likely exposed them to as many as twenty ads, most of them leading to high-risk sites offering gambling, get-rich-quick schemes, and the like. These kinds of sites are responsible for as much as 96 percent of the malware that's used by cybercriminals to access your machine in order to steal your information for various criminal enterprises. Learning to protect your kids and your machines go hand in hand.

The internet can create a false sense of privacy and community, with one-to-one conversations and anonymous screen names giving the illusion of a private space. Now, combine this with the natural tendency of teens everywhere to exaggerate, overshare, and test their boundaries, and you've got a recipe for all kinds of trouble.

CHECKING IN, CHECKING UP In 2016, 60 percent of parents with teenagers told the Pew Research Center that they'd checked out their teens' social media profiles and looked at the websites they visit, at least occasionally. And a similar percentage have friended or followed their teens on social media. About half of parents look at their teenager's phone call records or text messages, and know the passwords to their kids' phones.

Not surprising, younger parents are better at this—those under forty-five are much more likely to check up on teens and to check for the right stuff. For example, although every parent is worried about predators, younger parents are more likely to seek evidence of kids texting with unfamiliar friends and to look at call records and text records to ensure their kids aren't having inappropriate-sounding conversations with friends or strangers.

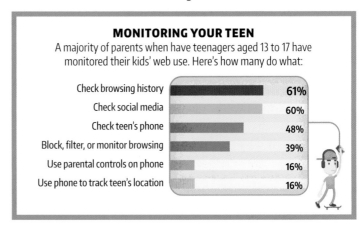

MONITORING YOUR TEEN

A majority of parents when have teenagers aged 13 to 17 have monitored their kids' web use. Here's how many do what:

Check browsing history	61%
Check social media	60%
Check teen's phone	48%
Block, filter, or monitor browsing	39%
Use parental controls on phone	16%
Use phone to track teen's location	16%

BAD DECISIONS All too often, teens are their own worst enemies. For example, a fair amount of inappropriate pictures actually originate with the teens themselves and then falls into the wrong hands. A kid may take selfies to share with a crush, assuming the images will stay private. Which they don't. The recipient might forward or share the pictures with friends, or might post the images as revenge after a breakup. And even if no one intentionally shares the pics, phones get stolen, iCloud accounts are hacked, and USB drives go missing.

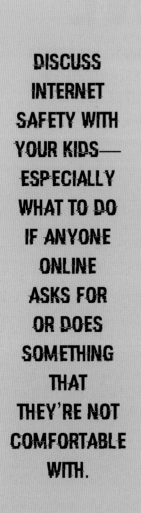

DISCUSS INTERNET SAFETY WITH YOUR KIDS— ESPECIALLY WHAT TO DO IF ANYONE ONLINE ASKS FOR OR DOES SOMETHING THAT THEY'RE NOT COMFORTABLE WITH.

The results can be tragic. Too many kids have tried suicide after such photos went public, often after vicious bullying. In some jurisdictions, teens have been prosecuted and branded for life as sex offenders for having nude photos of *themselves* on their phones.

Time for Real Talk This isn't a conversation any parent or child wants to have. But you need to, and keeping it fact-based is the key. Discuss real-life stories in the news, strategizing with your kids about how they'd handle these issues. Make it clear that many of the people hurt by online bullies or trolls didn't do anything wrong, but they still suffered.

KEY CONCEPT

STRATEGIC THINKING The specific online dangers change and evolve, but the tools kids need to combat them remain the same. A warning that stalkers may follow users on Instagram, or data on which online game has the most bullies, will date fast. Instead, encourage critical thinking by identifying the challenges and determining ways to avoid them. And always, *always* make it clear that you're there for them and will have their back.

BULLYING AND MOCKING Encourage kids to log, but not respond to, online bullying. If the bully persists, your child should feel comfortable coming to you for support. You should report it to school or police authorities.

REPUTATION ATTACKS Remind your kids that any private chat they have or image they share could go public. If they wouldn't want it posted on Facebook or mailed to Grandma, tell them to think twice before they hit "send."

PROFILING AND GROOMING If a new online friend suddenly starts commenting on your kid's Instagram, liking their Facebook posts, and retweeting them, be wary. This is often a precursor to asking for sexy pictures or more. Whether it's a cool-seeming stranger or a friend from school, teach your children to be careful.

TRUE STORY

CLOWNING AROUND In 2016, the United States. and the UK were gripped by what came to be known as the "clown scare." In multiple locations, several people claimed to have seen "evil clowns" menacing them. Schools received messages from social media accounts in which people dressed as clowns threatened to blow up schools or instigate shootings. Some schools closed for a day or more, went on high alert after receiving such threats. But once law enforcement got involved, it all unraveled pretty quickly. Officers looked at each clown's social media account, and determined who their first followers were. This gave the police names of the kids who made the profile, as well as their close friends. Those kids were shocked when, the day after they made an "anonymous" threat, police officers swooped in to make arrests for a number of felony-level charges.

MORE THAN 60 PERCENT OF TEENS SAY THAT THEIR TWEETS ARE PUBLIC. PREDATORS AND CRIMINALS CAN HARVEST A LOT OF INFORMATION FROM TWITTER, SO BE SURE YOUR KIDS LOCK DOWN THEIR SOCIAL MEDIA ACCOUNTS.

SORRY, NO KILLER APP Every marketing claim made by parental-control apps is more or less true, but there's no magic bullet. Indeed, many parents have found that the most rigorous parental control software is more annoying than it's worth. A smarter strategy involves securing your network and computers to a reasonable degree and then having more of those honest conversations with your kids about online safety.

Secure Your Network Your first step is to establish control of your Domain Name Servers (DNS). The DNS is the basic lookup tool used by everything on the internet to map a name to an IP address (which is a series of numbers, such as 208.67.220.220). We recommend setting your routers and devices to map to a DNS security site such as OpenDNS, which offers some basic free services that can help you control the sites your kids can visit, as well as premium options that allow for more customization. Your router may provide other parental control features as well, so check the specs online.

Secure Your Computers Remember, you're not protecting the computer from your kids. You're protecting your kids from danger. (Okay, fine, you're also protecting the computer from your kids.) Either way, you should password-protect your BIOS on Windows and Linux machines, or your firmware on a Mac, to prevent loading into bootable operating systems. If this sounds like gibberish, don't worry. Google the key terms and you'll find helpful step-by-step instructions (as well as helpful instructions for your kids on how to confound you—read those too!). Give your kids nonadministrative and highly locked-down user accounts so that they cannot install software or make changes without your approval. And, of course, choose a strong, almost-impossible-to-guess password.

Secure Your Kids This is the most likely point of failure. Remember, even if you successfully keep your children from accessing any "adult" sites, they can still be cyberbullied or stalked online by predators who know how to "groom" kids by empathizing with how mean and controlling their parents are. So, honesty is the best policy. These conversations should be age appropriate but specific: "There are bad people out there, and even though it feels as if you're anonymous on the internet, you're not." The point is not to scare them but rather to make them understand that the threats are real—and this isn't just you being overprotective.

SECURITY BASIC

MASTER OF YOUR DOMAIN You'd like to be able to trust that your kids are staying safe while using the internet, but just in case you need to keep an eye on them, there are ways. A home-based domain system (with its own URL) allows you to link multiple computers together and access information on a shared network, while bypassing your internet service provider to save on time and bandwidth. This whole mini-network can be protected from outside access with a firewall—and, properly configured, can also keep a log of any traffic going out to the internet, such as your kids' browsing history. The logs can record the time and date of the access, which device on the network it was done with, and the proper HTTP address and domain name, so you know where and when they're doing their browsing and with which mobile device or computer on your network. Plenty of companies offer services and software to build a home DNS, and there is no shortage of tutorials online that detail how to create your own.

GOOD TO KNOW

TAKE CONTROL When looking for parental-control software for your household, you'll find a range of options. Here are features we think are most important.

Be Inclusive Cover all platforms—Windows, Mac, iOS, and Android.

Set a Curfew Look for the ability to set times when the internet won't be available to the kids.

Stay in Control Look for remote management, monitoring, and control through a mobile app.

Know Now Set real-time alerts to text or email you if anyone tries to access a blocked site or search certain keywords.

Get Social Get your kid's social media logins and install software that alerts you to words or phrases and/or sends you random screen-grabs. Promise your kid you won't abuse your access, and keep that promise faithfully.

AGE-APPROPRIATE SURVEILLANCE When we use the word "surveillance," it's enough to make some parents cringe. Is that kind of thing really necessary? It sounds so . . . Orwellian. And what about letting kids make their own mistakes? Well, that's a nice idea when it comes to riding a bicycle or playing ice hockey, but on the internet it's possible to make mistakes that come at a serious cost. Kids have literally had their lives ruined as a result of something that started as harmless (to the kid) pranks. This isn't us being overly dramatic. Teens who send inappropriate photos can end up on a sexual predator registry for life, which greatly restricts the jobs they can have, where they can live, and more.

We believe that you really do have to surveil your kids, if only to keep track of their promises to you. This chapter gives you a basic tool kit. For how to apply it, the chart below is a good start. You're probably not monitoring your three-year-old's phone calls or keeping up to date on the permissions for the Curious George game your sixteen-year-old is still registered for. But other nuances may be a bit trickier.

CHILD'S AGE	INTERNET GUIDELINES	WHAT TO WATCH FOR	ANYTHING ELSE?
0–2	· No internet access. Instead, download educational games.	· Anything you didn't load yourself.	· Be aware that toddlers learn how to operate devices quickly so don't have anything on your phone or tablet that you don't want them to open.
3–4	· Install positive security controls (which allow you to spell out what to access; everything else is off limits). · Activate Google Safe Search. · Allow downloaded and single-player online educational games only.	· Anything you didn't load yourself. · Chat requests.	· Be sure you're acting as a positive role model for kids who are just getting started using the internet on their own.
5–7	· Practice shared online time. · Utilize kid-safe search engines.	· Read all emails. · Read chat content. · Be sure you recognize all chat partners. · Make sure nothing's getting through the Safe Search settings.	· Introduce kids to the idea of cyberbullying, and discuss how to protect against mean kids online. · Be sure to explain why oversharing is bad, while keeping the discussion age appropriate.

CHILD'S AGE	INTERNET GUIDELINES	WHAT TO WATCH FOR	ANYTHING ELSE?
8–10 	· Limit online time. · Set an audit trail through software or a router. · Limit social media. · Check social media interactions on all devices.	· Check your server and DNS logs regularly for inappropriate content or activity.	· Start talking about basic operational security (what not to reveal online, how to tell if someone might be a bad person, and so on).
11–13 	· Do more consistent social media monitoring. · Set up Google keyword search alerts.	· Inappropriate movies, gambling, meme, or image-sharing sites. · Pop-ups and adware. · Third-party toolbars and helpers. · Chat software.	· Time to have that awkward talk about adult content! · Keep talking about online security measures in more complex terms.
14–16 	· Monitor in-app purchases, set limits as necessary. · Monitor mobile hot spots. · Check on chat software; make sure you know every app your teen is using.	· Fake accounts. · Duplicate accounts. · USB-based OS. · Watch for "sneaking" of computer access. Check time logged on versus how much you actually see your kid using the computer.	· Begin conversations about family responsibility, such as protecting the house from theft. · Make sure your kid knows how to spot online predators. · Start talking about college applications and what your kid's social media profile conveys to those schools.
17+ 	· Check texts and IMs occasionally for inappropriate images or messages. · By now, you should have established a respectful, trusting relationship. Good job! But don't slack off until that kid is actually an adult.	· Malware activations. · Dual-boot or bootable OS sessions. · Virtual sessions. · TrueCrypt-style steganography. · Check browsing history: Your router or ISP may have DNS logs that differ from your browser's history (which can be scrubbed).	· Keep the conversations going; be sure to praise good behavior. · Review your teen's online footprint together; play the part of a college admissions officer or potential employer. · Do occasional Google searches of your kid's name.

GOOD TO KNOW

FIGHTING BLACKMAIL
One cruel trick played by predators is charming underage kids into sending pictures of themselves or luring them into a Skype call. Predators then use these images to blackmail the teen, asking for money or more photos and videos, threatening to send the original images to the kid's parents, school, or contacts list.

Reading this book puts you ahead of less-informed parents. Still, even smart, internet-savvy adults fall for online scams, and some creeps are frighteningly good at sweet-talking their way into a kid's confidences. Do your best to protect and inform your kids, and let them know that they can come to you if they get in trouble. Many kids are more scared of parents' anger or disappointment than they are of the blackmailer, and the results can be heartbreaking.

CASE STUDY

THAT AWKWARD TALK In a recent study, researchers found that 78 percent of high school students had watched inappropriate videos, beginning around the age of fourteen. That means that even if your kid hasn't looked for adult content on the internet, their friends may well be sharing jokes and memes about adult topics, often with no idea what they really mean. I'm not here to give you parenting advice, but I will share my story. As a cybercop, I probably realized what my son was looking at more quickly than the average parent. In the pages that follow, I'll talk about how we handled the tech aspects. That's the easy part.

As a father, I realized that I couldn't stop my kid from exploring the internet's back alleys, but I didn't want him to get some wrong ideas. And that led to a very awkward talk in which, while he fidgeted and blushed, I told him that I wasn't going to police his viewing. But I did want to be sure he knew to look at those images as movies, not real life. I told him that the performers are actors, and the scenes tell you as much about how real couples act as *Star Wars* does about the space program. I warned him that he might see stuff that is scary or gross, posted for shock value, and that I wouldn't get angry or disgusted if he wanted to ask me questions about things he saw. Time will tell, but I hope and trust I've done my part to raise a boy who knows the difference between fantasies and real human relationships.

AN HONEST APPROACH Kids will watch or download things you don't approve of. This is just reality. Every parent has a different threshold for what that might be, and that needs to be the beginning of a family discussion. It's important to realize that while most warnings focus on adult videos, particularly the more disturbing images a kid might stumble upon, it's not the only inappropriate stuff out there. Spend a few hours in some of the least savory corners of Reddit or 4chan, and you'll realize how hard it is to shield a child from the darker side of humanity. The solution, as we keep reiterating, is to have those honest conversations . . . and back them up with technological solutions.

DAD, IT'S BROKEN AGAIN I already discussed how I used my son's teenage surfing as a way to have a parenting moment. Every situation is different, but I think it always makes sense to explain to your kids why you don't want them looking at certain sites. Otherwise, you're just mean old dad or mom never letting them have any fun. Start out by talking about how criminals attract us with sexy pictures, promises of free games or movies, get-rich-quick schemes, and more. The more a link begs you to click on it, the less likely it is that it will deliver on its promise. So, point one, the cake is a lie. Explain to your kids that they shouldn't download that pirated expansion pack—not because stealing is wrong (although you can remind them that it is) but because that freebie is almost certainly infected with all kinds of computer-destroying malware.

My son managed to completely trash his computer more than once before it occurred to me to make him a deal: I would not only restore his machine (again!), I would back off on monitoring him (a little) if he installed VirtualBox on his computer and configured it to spin up a virtual instance of Windows that he could use as a one-time computer. Then he could watch whatever he wanted . . . but if we got one more virus, he'd lose computer privileges for six months.

It took him three days to figure out VirtualBox, and we've been virus-free ever since.

KEY CONCEPT

RANSOMWARE
Remember what we said earlier about the infecting your computer in as little as two clicks? Sometimes the software that gets downloaded to your computer doesn't just damage it or use it for someone else's purposes but actually hijacks your PC, locking you out or encrypting your files until you pay for a "software removal tool" or give in to outright extortion. Some "warnings" you might see on your screen are normally meant to trick you into accepting the ransomware. If you see such a pop-up message, immediately close the window or reboot to stop it from taking over. In a neat new twist, hackers have started ransoming other web-enabled devices, such as smart TVs. If it happens to you, try a hard restart to factory settings and, if that fails, contact the manufacturer. Some are claiming that this only happens if you download pirated materials, but the jury is still out.

TEACH YOUR KIDS TO BE GOOD INTERNET CITIZENS. EDUCATE THEM ON AVOIDING ANY ACTIONS THAT MIGHT HARM THEMSELVES OR OTHERS OR BREAK THE LAW.

HIDING BEHIND THE NET When my mother asked me to look over an email she'd gotten from her internet pen pal, I routed it immediately to my internal Raised Eyebrows Department. Don't get me wrong, I'm not saying Mom isn't a catch, but the way she described the burgeoning romance was enough to make me suspicious. She met the guy through a dating site and began to chat, then flirt, then send emails. And after a little while, he professed his love for her.

Grooming Behaviors The general pattern here is the same, whether people are targeting kids or adults and no matter what they're seeking. What's referred to as "grooming" is all about finding common ground with a likely target, gaining the person's trust, and then going in for the kill. With Mom's sweetie, all I had to do was select a particularly poetic-sounding sentence, cut and paste it into a Google search, and bingo. There was the same message from the same guy, in thousands of posts.

Rule One If an offer sounds too good to be true, I can pretty much guarantee that it absolutely is. If someone online promises your kids exactly what they want, teach them to be careful. They should ask, "Who does this person claim to be? Can this person prove it?" If the stranger is legit, this should not be difficult. Otherwise, instruct your teens to keep their antennas up.

Warning Signs Anyone who asks your child for photos right away is suspect. As is a new person who always seems to know when your kid logs in to certain applications. Or if the stranger mentions having money trouble. Or if your child suddenly starts getting pictures via email or text or Instagram—or any other way. Remember rule one. With your teen, try Googling a selection of text from the suspect emails—lots of these scammers work off of scripts and use the same emails over and over. Finally, if your teen asks to meet up and the person has a convoluted story about how they travel on business all the time, you can be certain that your kid is dealing with a fraud.

Con men use the internet's cloak of anonymity to steal money and maybe a heart or two. But online anonymity can mask an even more destructive face—that of the bully.

STAND UP TO CYBERBULLIES Bullying can be more serious than almost any other online offense. And all too often, victims are told, "Just ignore them." That was bad advice in the 1950s when the bullies were waiting to beat you up after school, and it's even worse advice when the bullying can come from multiple sources, online and off. Kids commit suicide every year because of bullying, and even adults have their lives turned upside down. (If you haven't read Amanda Nickerson's story, please do.)

If you or your children are targeted, contact authorities and do not accept no for an answer. Unfortunately, the internet can be rife with packs of bullies.

THE TAKEAWAY

Here's how to apply the lessons of this chapter to help keep your family safe from cyberbullies, online predators, and pesky malware..

BASIC SECURITY
- Monitor all social media accounts your child uses.
- Talk to kids about what's safe to share.

ADVANCED MEASURES
- Restrict and lock down your home network.
- Log traffic and use software to track net activity.
- Restrict social media sharing.
- Install GPS tracking apps on kids' phones.

TINFOIL-HAT BRIGADE
- Lock down all social media accounts to private.
- Use spyware to track all online activity.
- Use a private LAN for kids' computers and aggressively blacklist sites and categories at the router.

T/F

CYBER-BULLYING IS KIDS' STUFF

FALSE Cyberstalking, cyberbullying, and online smear campaigns are a growing and increasingly destructive form of abuse. It affects young and old, male and female, and even the famous: Jennifer Garner, Ellen Page, Ciara, 50 Cent, and a long list of other celebrities, have been cyberbullied and stalked or had private photos stolen and circulated. Comedian Leslie Jones took a break from Twitter after unrelenting racist and sexist abuse that began when she appeared in the remake of *Ghostbusters*. Social media sites have taken steps to stem the tide, but the most important step is to realize that anyone can be a victim.

THE INTERNET OF THINGS

THESE DAYS IT SEEMS LIKE EVERY GADGET, APPLIANCE, AND ACCESSORY IS "SMART" IN SOME WAY. THE INTERNET OF THINGS GIVES MORE POWER THAN EVER TO US AND OUR OBJECTS . . . AS WELL AS TO HACKERS AND SPIES.

A few years ago, the idea of a web-enabled clothes dryer or "smart" light bulb sounded like either marketing hype or really boring science fiction. Now, every new day seems to bring a new object that's been made "smarter." Sometimes the integration is subtle and virtually seamless—we've gone from watches to smart watches or Fitbits. Elsewhere, an upgrade solves a real problem in a helpful way. For example, video-enabled doorbells let you see who's at your door via a smartphone app, no matter where you are.

Internet-connected objects offer new powers and more control over our lives—who wouldn't want to turn off the stove from any room in the house, have the garage door open as you pull into the driveway, and keep that pesky neighborhood cat out while letting your cat in?

So, what's the catch? Well, what personal data is each device collecting? How is it stored? Is it secure? Has it ever been hacked? Do I need to update my password? (Pro tip: Companies are notoriously secretive about being hacked, for good reason.)

Smart objects are designed to make our lives better, to give us more control. But what if someone else takes control? For that matter, why hack a light bulb? Can a baby monitor be weaponized? What is my dryer saying about me to the fridge, anyway?

HOUSTON, WE HAVE BEVERAGES

The first internet-connected object, long before smart devices, was a humble vending machine. Back in 1982, computer science students at Carnegie Mellon found a solution to that age-old problem, the heartbreak of walking all the way to the soda machine only to find it's out of your favorite brand. That's fifteen minutes you'll never get back. Students Mike Kazar, David Nichols, John Zsarnay, and Ivor Durham installed microswitches in the vending machine and wrote a server program to report the machine's current status and temperature. That soda machine has become an internet legend and went on to inspire other projects, perhaps most notably the Trojan Room Coffee Pot at University of Cambridge, which, in 1991, used the world's first webcam so that students could see how much coffee was left in the pot without leaving their workstations.

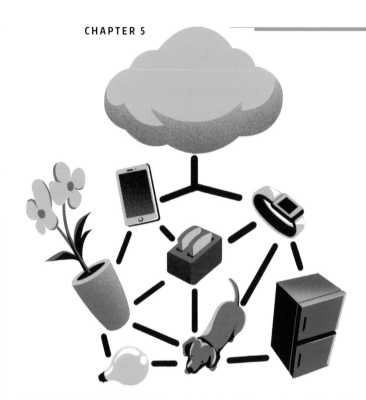

PHONE IT IN When we think of the ways smartphones have changed our lives, we tend to think of the convenience of texting, checking email, booking rides, and ordering takeout. We tend to forget that our phones are really small, powerful computers—and they're almost always online. BlackBerries and other internet-connected mobile devices before the iPhone existed were almost exclusively used for business. That changed in 2008 with the iPhone and its app store—and the countless apps developers could easily make for nearly everything. That drove demand for always-on internet and ubiquitous wireless access. Wi-Fi is often cheap or free and available mostly everywhere, and internet access is considered a basic human need on a par with water, heat, and electricity. In this world, it only makes sense that we'd control our homes, pets, and cars by phone.

A BRAVE NEW WORLD At its most utopian, IoT promises a futuristic home, with connected appliances you can control from your phone, thermostats that let you wake up to the perfect temperature, and light bulbs that turn themselves on in the morning and off at night. You can turn on the air conditioner in your smart car before you leave the beach so that the interior is refreshingly cool by the time you're ready to drive home. With a verbal command, devices in your home can play your favorite song, tell you the weather, or cue up a movie. Here are some of the "things" you might encounter.

Smarter Homes One of the richest sources of smart devices, homes have a staggering number of options for technological conveniences, and it increases every year—from smart coffee machines that will brew coffee when you wake up (based on a signal from your Fitbit) to internet-connected refrigerators, washing machines, dryers, and ovens. There's even an internet-connected sous vide that enables you to start that slow-cooking dinner from miles away. Pop your iPad into the docking station on your intelligent yoga mat, and you have a personal yoga teacher, without having to venture out of your home.

Smarter Cars Your home isn't the only thing getting smarter. If you've purchased a new car in the past few years, you know that its bells and whistles are all connected to the internet. Cars today come with their own internet connections and smartphone apps. Forgot where you parked? No worries, your smartwatch remembers!

Smarter Pets Most pets are microchipped—this makes it easy to reconnect with them if they get lost. But the "internet of pets" doesn't stop there! Radio-frequency identification (RFID) and microchip-activated pet doors only allow the pets you select to come and go. The problem with tag-related access is that pets can lose these tags, and they can be costly to replace. Got a pet that is overeating? The internet of pets can help with that, too, with smart feeding bowls.

Smarter You There are now plenty of wearable fitness trackers such as Fitbits or FuelBands, or Misfit fitness and sleep trackers. But internet-connected devices don't stop there. Smart medical devices already exist, and they're only getting smarter—like pacemakers or insulin pumps that can share your medical data with your doctor. Of course, these developments aren't without their own problems.

HOW PREVALENT IS SMART TECHNOLOGY IN U.S. HOMES?

As the internet of things weaves its wires throughout our lives, so too do objects in our homes become fully connected—and interconnected.

- Wireless speaker systems
- Smart thermostats
- Smart/wireless home security & monitoring systems
- Domestic robots (e.g. vacuum, lawnmower)
- Smart smoke/CO detectors
- Smart lighting
- Home energy use monitors
- Smart door locks
- Smart/connected refrigerator
- Smart/connected laundry machines
- Smart water detectors

OPTING OUT

There's really not much you can do to protect yourself from smart objects saving your data into the cloud and sharing it with the manufacturer. Here are a few hints for those worried about passive surveillance in their homes or businesses.

Study Up Read everything you can about the device you're interested in, particularly the manufacturer's data-use policies.

Hit Mute Opt out of passively collected data in your settings, if you can. You can use offline or airplane mode, which won't connect them to the internet—although you will be missing some functionality by doing so. Much of the point of these smart devices is to be connected to the internet.

Change Passwords Be sure to change the default passwords on your devices and routers.

COSTS OF CONNECTIVITY Who wouldn't want all this neat stuff? Besides the sometimes high price tags, what are the downsides?

Unsecured Data Much of this technology is still so new that the bugs are still being worked out . . . or surfacing unexpectedly. After all, Bluetooth and smartphone apps are great tools, but they were never designed to safeguard confidential information. As voice command becomes more common, most folks haven't yet wondered whether Alexa ever stops listening. If the microphones are always on, and the internet connection always live, what's happening to all that data? Is anybody listening? And if so, who are they and what are they capable of? There are lots of questions, and the answers are only just now being made public.

Listening Ears In today's competitive business environment, the "consumer data use revenue model" is a big sell point for any digital entrepreneur looking for funding to launch a new product or company. In other words, most new trackers and sensors have a plan to use the data they collect on you for other purposes—for example, to sell to marketers. Some have even more nefarious uses.

The Bottom Line The problem with filling our world with smart objects and sensors—although they will absolutely help us have better lives—is a data problem. We need to ask what data is being collected, how secure the storage servers are, how that data will be used, and who ultimately owns it. Right now, data collection, use, and ownership stays with the business that makes the product. Most businesses are motivated by money—and your data is money.

Then there are other problems with these devices. Recently, I wanted to turn on my Hue connected light bulbs. But before I could do so, I was forced to update my software—turning a swipe into a five-minute update! While a Nest thermostat is fantastic for remotely monitoring and controlling the heating and cooling in my home, hacks giving access to my data could make my home a target for thieves. The Nest could even be tampered with to spy on me!

These devices may be smart, but they don't have morals. Where most people would feel uncomfortable listening in on private conversations in private homes, these objects have no such ethical guidelines built into them. It's the people who work at the manufacturers who decide what is fine to listen in on, what data to store, how to store it, and what to do with it.

GOOD TO KNOW

WHAT A DOLL! Science fiction is chock-full of stories about kids' intelligent toys being used for good or evil. This concept has moved another step closer to reality with the coming wave of toys that use Bluetooth and a phone app to communicate with children. One of the first "smart" dolls was My Friend Cayla, who connects to the internet and relays information provided by a child, something like a cuter version of Siri with some parental controls. More sophisticated options include Hello Barbie, a model of the world-famous doll that uses pre-scripted lines to communicate with a child while also building a cloud-based bank of information to better tailor those conversations to that individual. Concerns about these toys include uncertainty about what information is stored, how it will be used, and how secure it is from theft. In addition, hackers have found that they're able to hijack the Bluetooth signal that controls Barbie from outside a home and "speak" whatever they please to kids in the doll's voice.

KEY CONCEPT

HIJACKED DEVICES
Your data isn't the only thing at risk if hackers break in to your devices. They can also use them to attack websites. These Distributed Denial of Service (DDoS) attacks happen when computers or other internet-linked devices are programmed to repeatedly request a specific website. The millions of requests from hacked devices overwhelm the server, causing the site to go down. In 2016, malware called Mirai (Japanese for "future") used IoT connectivity to launch a massive DDoS attack. It identified over sixty default user names and passwords and took over devices such as baby monitors, DVRs, and security cameras, in a network called a botnet. In October 2016, this botnet hit DNS service provider Dyn, as well as PayPal, Spotify, Wired, GitHub, Twitter, Reddit, Netflix, Airbnb, and others. At least 1.2 million IoT devices are possibly still infected by Mirai.

HOME SWEET CYBERHOME

Unless you have a love affair with high-tech gadgets and a salary to match, your home may not be quite this wired. That said, you may well have more connections to the internet of things than you realize. As IoT technology gets cheaper and more ubiquitous, more and more devices will be talking to each other.

PEOPLE
- Bluetooth headset
- Fitness tracker
- Smartphone
- Smartwatch
- Medical device
- Hearing aid
- Baby w/ smart diaper

BEDROOM
- Smart mattress (sleep tracker)
- Intelligent yoga mat

KIDS ROOM
- Baby monitor
- Smart doll
- Nanny cam bear

LAUNDRY, UTILITY ROOM
- Washer
- Dryer
- Vacuum cleaner

GARAGE
- Vehicle (with GPS, stereo, Bluetooth phone connectivity)
- Garage door
- Smart lawnmower
- Water heater

LIVING ROOM, STUDY, ETC
- Nest/ thermostat/AC
- Entertainment system/TV
- Personal computer
- Game console
- Smart TV
- Exercise equipment (elliptical, treadmill)
- Pet door (synced to pet's collar)

EVERYWHERE IN GENERAL
- CO & smoke detectors
- Wireless speakers
- Smart light bulbs
- Smart heating vents (open and close to shift heat to cooler areas)

BATHROOM
- Smart scale
- Smart mirror
- Toothbrush
- Smart breathometer (tells you if you have bad breath)

KITCHEN
- Fridge
- Coffee maker
- Sous vide
- Dishwasher
- Oven/range

EXTERIOR
- Lights
- Cameras
- Door/window alarms
- Sprinklers
- Front door (pet door too; see above, left)

TRUE STORY

BAD VIBRATIONS How personal is the data your devices might be sending to manufacturers, with or without your consent? There are two big problems for smart tool users: Manufacturers tend to put little effort into security, and they may be gathering data without your knowledge. In 2016, hackers at DEF CON decided to hack a personal smart tool as a conversation starter about assault. They weren't surprised at how easy it was to take over the device, but what was unexpected and shocking was that it was secretly gathering data on the user's favorite settings and other factors and uploading them to the company.

GETTING SMARTER ABOUT SMART DEVICES "Smart object," "smart device," "internet-connected device"—these are all terms that are used to describe objects that connect to and use the internet. Some devices connect directly to the internet from your home network through your router, while others connect to the internet via an app on your smartphone. When these devices are connected to the internet, you're able to remotely control them—or program them to do things on their own. Say, for example, you want to schedule your lights to turn on at dusk, whether you're at home or not. Smart light bulbs become smarter when connected to a weather site that provides the time of sunset. There are websites with hundreds of these kinds of programs.

Making Smart Objects Even Smarter IFTTT (which stands for "if this, then that") is a free web-based service that allows you to create applets that enable you to connect your smart devices together. This presents an interesting range of security advantages but also concerns. The biggest concern is, what if someone managed to hack IFTTT? The way data is stored makes it unlikely that a breach would give hackers access to vast amounts of data or control of all your devices. Still, it is a worry for some. A more immediate concern is the tendency for oversharing. The more data about your movements you put out there, the more opportunities there are for someone to track you for nefarious purposes.

On the other hand, many IFTTT applets are specifically designed to make you, your home, and your family more secure. The table on the facing page depicts a number of these options to show you how versatile IFTTT can be. Do the security and convenience of these applets outweigh concerns about hackers? Only you can make that call, but the possibilities are intriguing.

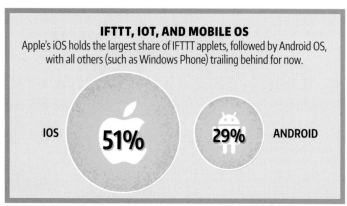

IFTTT, IOT, AND MOBILE OS
Apple's iOS holds the largest share of IFTTT applets, followed by Android OS, with all others (such as Windows Phone) trailing behind for now.

IOS **51%**　　**29%** ANDROID

IF THIS . . .		. . . THEN THAT
Security camera recognizes a face at the front door		Porch lights turn on
Vehicle approaches garage and Bluetooth system is recognized		Garage door opens
Pet (wearing smart collar) gets close to pet door		Pet door opens
Doorbell is rung		Security camera sends picture of visitor to smartphone
Last person leaves house		House confirms oven is off and sends that person a text
Sun rises (or sets)		Blinds on sun-facing side of house close (or open)
Smoke alarm goes off		Next-door neighbor receives text message on smartphone
No inhabitants are detected inside home		Security cameras and alarms activate
Wake-up alarm goes off in the morning		Coffee maker in kitchen turns on
A door or window is forced open		A security camera sends a photo and text to smartphone
An inhabitant in the house moves from one room to another		Air vents close in previous room and open in new room
No inhabitants are detected inside room		Roomba activates and begins cleaning the floor

GOOD TO KNOW

ACCESS GRANTED With all these concerns about data privacy, there is some good news: Plenty of companies are now working on technical solutions to help enable more control and security with data sharing. UMA, which stands for User-Managed Access, is an OAuth 2.0 protocol that defines how developers can enable a smart object to engage in secure selective data sharing. This protocol makes it easier for developers of software and hardware to let the owner of the smart device specify what data they would like to share and what to keep restricted. The use of UMA removes the security burden from the item's manufacturer and also gives consumers or owners more power over the proliferation of their own data. UMA is a protocol that can be used right now, in fact—we just need to get more manufacturers to use it in their products. Look for it when you buy, for greater safety.

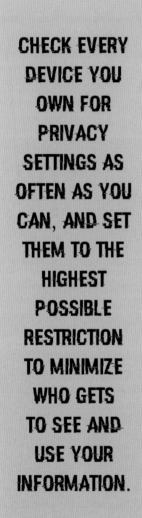

CHECK EVERY DEVICE YOU OWN FOR PRIVACY SETTINGS AS OFTEN AS YOU CAN, AND SET THEM TO THE HIGHEST POSSIBLE RESTRICTION TO MINIMIZE WHO GETS TO SEE AND USE YOUR INFORMATION.

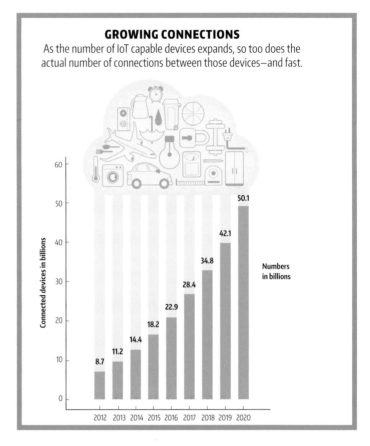

GROWING CONNECTIONS
As the number of IoT capable devices expands, so too does the actual number of connections between those devices—and fast.

Connected devices in billions

Numbers in billions

Year	Value
2012	8.7
2013	11.2
2014	14.4
2015	18.2
2016	22.9
2017	28.4
2018	34.8
2019	42.1
2020	50.1

UNDER SURVEILLANCE All around us, data is collected about our activities and behavior. From what route we took to get to the grocery store (Waze, Google Maps) to whom we're messaging (Facebook Messenger, WhatsApp), companies that build the software we use are constantly tracking and monitoring us. Much of it is used for what's called "surveillance marketing."

May Be Relevant to Your Interests Surveillance marketing happens when companies such as Google, Facebook, Amazon, and other sites observe the information (data) you generate by using their services. Google was a pioneer in this field with what was then called "contextual marketing" back in the early 2000s. After the release of Gmail, Google began monitoring the contents and context of messages in order to show advertising based on all of those messages. If you emailed your mom about an upcoming vacation to Bali, Google might show you ads about airfare specials, travel, or vacation activities in the South Pacific. After some outcry, the company put a halt to this particular practice. But it's still the case that if you search shopping sites for the perfect pair of rain boots you'll likely be stalked by advertisements for rain boots for the next year or so, across a range of sites.

Information, Please Data is collected about you not just on the Web but when also you use your phone and smart devices. Your smart thermostat, your car, your light bulbs, and your fitness tracker are spying on you and reporting back to . . . someone. Imagine the offline version of this—a company representative listening in on your private conversations and following you around to see what you buy You wouldn't stand for that kind of behavior in the real world, but it's become part of what you expect online.

Big Brother Wants to Watch The internet of things (especially IFTTT devices) works by monitoring and responding to everything you do. But this also means that someone else could be watching. In 2016, former FBI director of national intelligence James Clapper informed a Senate panel that the government had known about the potential to use IoT and IFTTT to spy on their users. Privacy advocates, in response, are encouraging consumers to use end-to-end encrypted smart devices and are pushing for more privacy laws.

KILLER APP

DITCH THAT TAIL If a creepy dude is following you, you can duck into a safe space to escape. But online spies aren't immediately visible, so how do you ditch them? If you want to minimize instances of being tracked online, use an ad blocker such as Adblock Plus and site tracking browser plug-ins such as Ghostery. But beware, some sites will intentionally offer less functionality or ban your browsing outright if you use an ad blocker. If you are concerned about Facebook using your personal data (or any apps that you have given access to your Facebook data), remove Facebook Messenger from your smartphone, and use a secure messaging system such as Signal, Wickr, or SMS. And if you want to stay truly stealthy, you can always use Tor.

T/F

A SMART APPLIANCE WAS WITNESS TO A MURDER

TRUE (kind of) All police knew in late 2015 was that Victor Collins and James Bates had spent an evening soaking in Bates's hot tub listening to music streamed by an Amazon Echo. According to Bates, he went to bed early. When he woke up in the morning, Collins had apparently drowned.

Police were suspicious, and it quickly became clear that Collins was in a fight before his death and had likely been drowned. But there was no witness. Or was there?

Investigators served a warrant to Amazon, hoping the Echo had recorded anything of interest. It's unlikely that Alexa will take the stand, but an interesting precedent may have been set. Siri, where's the best place to bury a body?

- - - - - ● - - - - -

T/F

YOU CAN HACK A PACEMAKER

TRUE While this is true, it hasn't happened to a person—yet. Many medical devices have wireless functionality to share information with your doctor to see how well the device is working. The late hacker Barnaby Jack did pioneering work here, and in 2016, security firm MedSec hacked pacemakers and defibrillators and then licensed to a Wall St. hedge fund the data on how they did it. Medsec's hacks included sending a shock—wirelessly. The firm shorted the stock of the manufacturer, St. Jude Medical. St. Jude denied this, but the FDA and DHS confirmed the hacks. Barnaby's most famous hack had been of an insulin pump, causing delivery (in a lab) of a lethal dose of insulin.

- - - - - - - - -

ON THE ROAD As the internet of things grows, it's no surprise that it extends to affect our vehicles as well. Our cars, trucks, and SUVs are not only a source of more data for companies to mine but open drivers up to a new range of threats.

Digital Carjacking In 2015, *Wired* magazine writer Andy Greenberg volunteered to drive a Jeep Cherokee while hackers attempted to control it remotely. Hackers Charlie Miller and Chris Valasek were able to take control from ten miles away by laptop; Greenberg was helpless to stop the duo from controlling the A/C, radio, windshield wipers—and even stopping the transmission. The same sort of vulnerability had been demonstrated previously in 2013, with hackers accessing the brakes, horn, seat belt, and steering wheel of a Toyota Prius with Greenberg behind the wheel. Only in recent years have legislators begun to set electronic security standards for automobiles, and some auto makers have issued even recalls for their vehicles. Nonetheless, the risk of hackers assuming control to control it, stalk the driver, or steal relevant data still exists. So far, the hacks have only been done to help understand a car's vulnerabilities. However, it is no longer the stuff of bad movies to imagine that you could be hurtling down the freeway when, with no warning, your doors lock, brakes fail, steering freezes, and seat belt clicks open. But hey, you can still stream your Spotify playlist, so that's good.

Driverless Cars Anyone who has been paying attention knows that the era of the driverless car is finally upon us, as more and more companies follow in the steps of Google's extensive testing. Safety concerns are, of course, paramount, and there have been a number of fender benders (mainly the driverless car being rear-ended by a car with a driver inside), along with reports of cars blowing through red lights or stop signs. A Tesla in "autopilot" (semi-driverless) mode was involved in a fatal accident back in 2015, but after much investigation, the manufacturer was absolved of fault. Indeed, the statistics show that cars with autopilot are actually involved in 40 percent fewer incidents.

THE TAKEAWAY

As the internet of things is a relatively new phenomenon, ways of keeping yourself safe mainly involve doing your research and using common sense.

BASIC SECURITY

- Research purchases before you buy.
- Change your modem and router passwords to something other than the factory default.
- Use screen lock codes on all mobile devices.
- Isolate IoT apps.

ADVANCED MEASURES

- Ensure that medical devices are locked to only critical services.
- Ask device providers about wireless security.

TINFOIL-HAT BRIGADE

- Set up a separate home network with a separate firewall with all your IoT Devices behind the firewall.
- Place IoT devices on a virtual LAN segment.
- Install surveillance software to collect data packets sent from your devices through your network.

FUN FACT

FLYING THE UNFRIENDLY SKIES

Not all the problems surrounding smart vehicles and devices are limited to the ones that are on the ground. Radio hackers have broken into American and British air traffic control and transmitted bogus flight information to pilots. These "ghost transmissions" have requested that pilots change their landing plans and diverge from flight paths. Up until now, the instances of air traffic hacking have been low in number; only twenty ghost transmissions have been properly identified and no one has ever been caught in the act, let alone prosecuted. The equipment for breaking into the pilot's signal sets a user back about $450 USD—still well within the means of a determined troublemaker. And the real problem is that there's currently no technology available to block the unauthorized people who are making these transmissions.

NOT JUST PHONING IT IN

NEVER MIND THAT YOUR SMARTPHONE IS MORE POWERFUL THAN THE COMPUTERS THAT POWERED THE SPACE SHUTTLE. THE REAL ISSUE WITH PHONES IS THAT THEY CONTAIN A COMPLETE SET OF THE METADATA OF YOUR LIFE.

The era of pocket-sized computers predicted since the 1950s began in earnest in 2007 with the release of the first iPhone. Today, people all over the planet carry with them at all times a device capable of accessing the internet, the Global Positioning System, and hundreds of millions of nearby devices. We've passed the point of inflection: More people these days view websites with their mobile phone than on desktop or laptop computers.

We entrust to our phones more data than we traditionally stored on our home computers. Our phones know exactly where we are and where we've been, and can tell exactly where we're going. They know how much we have in our bank account and what we've bought on Amazon; they can open our front doors and start our cars; they know how much dirt is on our floors and whether our smoke alarm batteries are charged. They can transmit and receive voice and text communications between us and anyone else in the world. They know, increasingly, whether we need to buy a quart of milk or how many people read that story we posted on Facebook. Golly, that's a lot of data about us. Say, these phones are secure, right?

Well, not really. In fact . . . if you're not very careful, your phone can cause you some serious problems.

PIKACHU, I CHOOSE YOU! You may have seen one futuristic thriller or another, wherein the bad guys use some clever or disgusting method to breach security using a victim's thumbprint. But as it turns out, you don't need to be a supervillain or a high-tech professional to be a cyberthief. In 2016, the *Wall Street Journal* reported the story of a six-year-old who used her sleeping mother's thumbprint to unlock the mom's phone. She then went on to order $250 USD worth of Pokémon toys from Amazon. When her parents received thirteen different order confirmations they assumed their account had been hacked—until their daughter proudly announced that she'd been shopping just like Mommy. Parents of precocious children might want to rethink their password strategies, wear gloves while napping, or just make sure their smartphones are kept safely out of reach.

BASIC PHONE SETTINGS So, you've just gotten a new phone! Congratulations. As you set it up, you should keep some things in mind in order to make security a basic part of the way you operate your phone from the beginning, as opposed to trying to patch it up later.

Lock It Down First, enable your phone's "Lock SIM Card" option, which will require a password to access your SIM card every time that the phone is rebooted. This is in addition to your phone's screen lock. The SIM lock secures the network access card, while the screen lock protects the phone itself.

Secure Your Screen Next, enable your phone's screen lock to keep snoops, busybodies, and evildoers from going through your stuff. If you can use a password or passphrase (instead of a PIN), do it. If you use a PIN, make it six numbers or longer. Set the lock timer low enough to ensure that it automatically secures itself when you leave it in a restaurant or in a taxi, but long enough to avoid entering your passcode every three seconds—two minutes should be a good degree of compromise.

Fingers Off! Plenty of smartphone models offer fingerprint detection as a quick way of unlocking and accessing your phone, but despite its convenience, you should deactivate that setting completely and rely on PINs and passwords for your privacy and protection.

Stay Cryptic Deactivate location settings unless you specifically need them. Often you'll end up needing to turn location on for specific apps when you need it—say to get driving directions—but it's worth the (relatively minimal) trouble.

Use Only What You Need You should also turn off your phone's Wi-Fi, tethering, hot spot, Bluetooth, and near-field communication settings. All of these are useful, but you should only activate them as you need them rather than simply leaving them on by default.

THE BEST WAY TO ASSURE YOUR PRIVACY AND SECURITY IN CASE YOUR PHONE IS LOST OR STOLEN IS TO SET A GOOD PASSCODE OR SECURITY PATTERN—AS COMPLEX AS YOU CAN MAKE IT.

Block Out Finally, consider blocking your phone's caller ID to maintain maximum privacy. The people you call will see you on their end as "Unknown" or "Private Caller" and as a result some of them will no doubt ignore your calls. This is a borderline "Advanced" or even "Tin Foil Hat Brigade" level of security, for those who really want to go stealth. You're going to be leaving a lot of voicemails, since most "private callers" are debt collectors, scammers, doctors' offices, and cops.

GOOD TO KNOW

In this chart, apps in tan are generally configured to protect your privacy. Items in yellow can be safe so long as you watch your settings and understand what you are trading for fun or convenience. Items in orange are known to have poor privacy controls and/or to sell user information to advertisers or the government.

APP OR FEATURE	EXAMPLES
SECURE MAIL	K-9, Proton, SafeMail for Gmail, Inky
PRIVACY APPS	Ghostery; Dash VPN; TorGuard VPN; Orfox: Tor Browser for Android; Orbot: Proxy with Tor; Red Onion
SECURE CHAT	Signal, WhatsApp, Wickr
TRANSPORTATION	Uber, Lyft
SOCIAL MEDIA	Facebook, Twitter, Instagram, Kik, Reddit, Vine, Tumblr
SPYING SOFTWARE	FlexiSPY, mSpy
GAMES	Fruit Ninja, Angry Birds, Despicable Me, Words with Friends
FLASHLIGHT	Flashlight, Brightest Flashlight

SECURITY BASIC

FIND MY PHONE
There have been, over the past few years, a number of high-profile cases in which users have located their stolen smartphones (both iOS and Android) or tablet through "find my phone" applications. These are generally a good idea to have running because as it turns out, petty or nonprofessional thieves are generally not that careful when it comes to using stolen phones— they just turn them on and use them. Duh.

When your phone is stolen, be sure to go to the police station and fill out a theft report. When you locate your stolen phone, you don't want the first conversation with the fuzz to be about your phone having been stolen. Rather, you want to say, "Hey! You know that phone I reported stolen in report MP1735068? I found it! It's at 356 Main Street." That has a better chance of success in terms of getting the cops to help you retrieve your device.

GOOD TO KNOW

WHAT'S IN YOUR SMARTPHONE? A wise man may have once claimed, "You are not the contents of your wallet," but that was before smartphones came along. Your wallet probably has a few pictures, some cash, and a range of cards: identification, insurance, debit, and credit. All of these are meaningful and should be replaced if your wallet is lost or stolen, but it doesn't compare at all to what your smartphone can contain: Hundreds of photographs and videos, hundreds or even thousands of emails, open apps with personal info such as banking, passwords to every online account you have, as well as continuous access to any and all further sensitive information sent to those accounts. In short, you are the contents of your phone to anyone who steals or breaks into it. Keep it even closer to you and more secure than your wallet.

YOUR PHONE IS NOT A WALLET . . . EXCEPT WHEN IT IS Your mobile phone is not inherently unsafe, but you will need to understand the relative risk that a given app presents and compare that to the reward you get by using it. When you think about using a new app, consider the following: What do I get, and what does it cost me, really?

It's the same as giving your personal information to supermarkets in exchange for a frequent shopper card. You enjoy savings, but the store maintains a complete dossier on what you buy—and don't. They know the days you go shopping and the amount they can count on you to spend, and they have a good idea about how to increase that amount. That data is theirs to do with as they please, and they often sell it to the highest bidder.

Banking on You When your bank asks you to try its new app, they obviously want you to use it because it teaches them more about you. What's the risk? The bank will always pay back your losses if the app gets breached. If you find it convenient to deposit checks from your phone or transfer money, that's a great deal. But you need to understand what you are giving them and the cost of the worst-case scenario. Is Google Wallet or Apple Pay as convenient as Google and Apple make it sound? It depends on your circumstances—if you live in a big city, sure; out in the country? Probably not.

What Do You Need? Do you have a nine-year-old who uses your phone for multiplayer online gaming, or is this a business phone with a few key applications and a good password? Everyone's needs are different, and one man's convenience is another man's big shiny target. Give some serious thought to what you want to get from your apps and how you use your devices. For example, use a different mobile device for sensitive apps like banking, and only use the device for that—this gives you much of the convenience but with less risk.

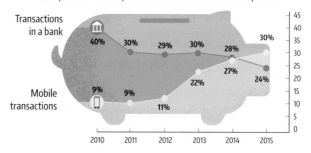

THIS LITTLE PIGGY WENT ONLINE
In the past couple of years, the number of people who bank using their phones has outpaced the number who bank in person.

Transactions in a bank: 40% 30% 29% 30% 28% 30%

Mobile transactions: 9% 9% 11% 22% 27% 24%

2010 2011 2012 2013 2014 2015

You probably have a pretty good grasp of your phone's basic features, but it may still be able to surprise you with what it can do—and how it can affect your data safety. Here are some possible security risks you might want to check out.

FEATURE	WHAT IT'S FOR	WHAT YOU SHOULD KNOW	WHAT TO DO
GPS	LOCATION AND DIRECTIONS	Your GPS provides your location to any app in the phone—including apps you might not know about. Some phones keep records of where you have been stored in a file on the phone and uploaded to the cloud . . . somewhere.	Be selective in granting permission to apps to use your location. Shut off location services unless you are actively using them for something.
WIFI	INTERNET CONNECTIVITY	You often need Wi-Fi to cut down on mobile data use, but Android phones use Wi-Fi to more exactly locate you. By sensing the relative strength of available Wi-Fi hot spots, they can triangulate your position much more closely than with GPS alone.	Keep Wi-Fi turned off unless you're using it; deny permission to "Use Wi-Fi to enhance your location."
CAMERA	SHOOTING PHOTOGRAPHS OR VIDEO	Your phone can add metadata to your photographs, including the location, time and date, and other personal information.	Look in your phone's settings to limit the metadata added to photos or EXIF data.
FACEBOOK	SOCIAL NETWORKING	Facebook takes about as many liberties with your personal data as anyone outside Fort Meade.	Only you can make the risk/benefit analysis as to whether Facebook's juice is worth the squeeze of handing Facebook all your data.
MICROPHONE	SPEAKING, RECORDING	Your phone's microphones (there are often more than one) are high-quality directional and omnidirectional mics capable of grabbing crisp, clear audio. Any hack that grabs your mic can use it as a very powerful listening device.	This is the hardest to mitigate. Tin Foil Hat Brigade members recommend removing your phone's mic entirely and using a lanyard mic such as the one that comes with your earbuds.
BANKING APP	MONEY MANAGEMENT	Banking apps can be very convenient. They have also been hacked, forcing data to be forwarded to places you might not want.	Be careful about using these tools, and never for business (banks don't have to reimburse business accounts after fraud).

ERIC OLSON ON METADATA: The best way to think about metadata is that it is data describing other data. A movie review blurb like "A delightful yarn," could be considered to be metadata about a two-hour movie in which a clever and complicated story is told. Metadata is a high-level description or abstraction that gives you an understanding of the data itself. If I'm standing in a bookstore, and I've got to give my boss a report tomorrow, I'm wondering which of these books contains the content I need, and there may be eleven factors I'm considering: Does the book fit in my briefcase? Do I know the author? Are they a trusted source? Is this thing too heavy to hold up while I'm in the bathtub?

All those are factors about the book that have nothing to do with the content in the book. So, for each datum, there's the message or content of the datum itself, and there's a whole range of information around it that is about it but not that which is in it.

Listening In If we look at the metadata in the context of phones, we see that it can be incredibly powerful. The best known example is the government looking at metadata of your phone calls. If you receive a phone call from a doctor or a blood lab and speak for three minutes, then you call a pharmacy and speak for two minutes, and then you

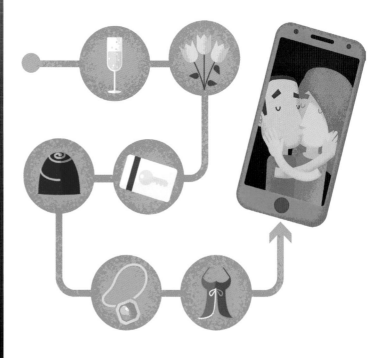

call an AIDS patient advocacy group and speak for nineteen minutes, the government might consider it likely that you've just gotten a diagnosis of HIV.

Similarly, if you should receive a call from a known drug dealer lasting for a minute or two, and then follow it up by making a set of calls to three of your friends and speaking with each for under two minutes, this might lead investigators to believe that you have just agreed to buy drugs and to share them with your friends.

Learning Your Habits Metadata needn't be about legal matters; it can describe lifestyle choices and behaviors. Imagine if your health insurance company had access to call metadata or the information from your supermarket's club card, so it could base your rates on how often you ordered Chinese takeout or how many frozen pizzas you bought—or whether or not you've renewed your gym membership?

Simple Summaries Metadata needn't be complicated; in fact, one single character can provide a wealth of information. For example, your grade of B in a class is metadata describing an entire semester of your work. It's long been used to identify kids in need of extra help in school. An entry of 1 instead of a 0 in a field like "gun owner" can change the way the police approach a house or car. Of course, such a simplistic on/off bit of metadata can occasionally be subject to error, especially when entered initially by a human user—consider the aforementioned example of whether the police believe you to be a gun owner when approaching your house or car.

It's All in How You Use It Despite all this, though, there are actually more good uses than bad of metadata—meta-analysis (the aggregation and analysis of metadata from multiple sources), for example, is probably the best way to understand the overall efficacy of a drug—have a look at the Cochrane Collaboration (http://www.cochrane.org/), and you can understand how examination and aggregation of the metadata around drug trials can help produce better health outcomes. Metadata, like technology, is a dual-use issue. Its "goodness" or "badness" depends on the context and your perspective. —Eric Olson

TRUE STORY

THE FBI VS. APPLE

Public debate over law enforcement access to phones came to a head after the FBI sought, under the All Writs Act, to force vendors to provide cops with a "backdoor" to encrypted iPhones. The case arose after the FBI sought possible evidence on the iPhone used by a mass shooter in San Bernardino who attacked a government office in December of 2015.

The FBI sought to force Apple to break the strong encryption of that device. Apple refused, arguing that a backdoor was the same as a master key for cops. The police argued that Apple was creating a safe space for criminals.

Finally, the FBI bought a tool from hackers to break the protection on the iPhone and get the data they sought. The argument is not yet over; both sides are still waiting for a great test case, ultimately to be settled by the United States Supreme Court.

TRUE STORY

SELLING YOUR SMARTPHONE'S SOUL

Some apps are notable for doing a lot more than you were expecting when you downloaded an installed them. A now-famous smartphone flashlight, for example, is the poster child for this kind of unwelcome surprise. The Brightest Flashlight app, estimated by the Federal Trade Commission to have been downloaded tens of millions of times, stole identifying data, location, calendar information, camera and microphone access, email, and network surveillance—essentially giving your whole phone to the app. The app makers were then selling all this information to advertisers. The lesson? If you decide to install an external app, examine the permissions that it asks for. Use apps that only ask for permissions related to their tasks. If an app is suspect, ask questions, or look for one that uses fewer permissions.

IS THAT JAMES BOND IN YOUR POCKET, OR ARE YOU JUST HAPPY TO SEE ME? When people with national security clearances enter Secure Compartmentalized Information Facilities (SCIF)—the secure rooms we have seen in the movies—all mobile phones are confiscated. If a phone is detected, the owner is in huge trouble. This is because of the fact that as phones get better, they offer really neat spy tools that many people forget they have handy at all times.

Utilize Electronic Eavesdropping Want to record a meeting? There's an app for that. Leave your phone on the table, with its screen turned off, and you can covertly get a high-fidelity stereo recording of what's being said. There are also free or low-cost apps that record all incoming an outbound calls, spoof your number to whatever you want it to be, detect mobile networks and cellular signals, and do several other cool tricks as well.

Keep Track of a Subject Would you like to spy on someone else's phone? If you have access to it (and flexible morals) you can easily download and install apps that can track, say, your significant other or your kids. If you have no morals whatsoever, you can place spyware on the phone of a coworker or your employer, for a little industrial espionage. Of course, this works both ways: Your employer can place spyware on your phone and probably be within the law in several states, so long as he or she owns the phone. Spyware can allow you to, for example, remotely activate the microphone on a phone and listen in on the conversation or access the GPS to both track location and set up a geo-fence, which will send you a text message when your quarry leaves a designated area.

Steal Secrets If you've set up spyware on someone else's phone (or someone has done

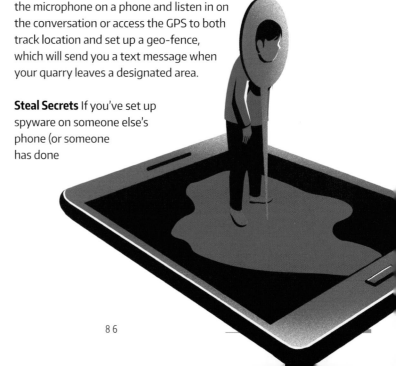

it to your phone instead), you can also peek in on social media accounts, snatch the very keys they type with a keylogger, crack passwords, and access other wonderful features. You have a robust piece of covert surveillance gear that used to require a boxy suit and a mustache to twirl—or at the very least, nation-state funding.

Don't Just Make Calls We as users continue to get it wrong, seeing smartphones as "phones" and not "computers." They are decidedly the latter, and they're capable of doing all the things a computer can do—we should never to forget that.

KILLER APP

A number of apps can help you feel more secure, whether you fear for your civil liberties or your wallet. It's definitely a good idea to check out the iTunes or Google Play Store regularly to learn about new applications—just use the keywords "safety," "spyware," and the like. Read the reviews online to learn about possible vulnerabilities and to find the best functionality for your needs, and always check the permissions when installing and app.

Electronic Frontier Foundation The EFF's app updates you on civil liberty issues and helps you tweet to government leaders.

ACLU The American Civil Liberties Union lets you record police activity and upload it in real time to a cloud server to document police abuses or brutality.

bSafe Personal Safety This, and similar apps, can identify people in your network to help you stay safe, travel in groups, and get help.

Other Safety and Privacy Apps Many personal-safety apps are also available, both from cities (such as the BART safety app for riders of the San Francisco Bay Area transit system) as well as private concerns (such as the ICE—In Case of Emergency—app)

SECURITY BASIC

KEEPING A SECURE CONNECTION Your smartphone's Wi-Fi and Bluetooth capabilities mean you can connect anywhere, anytime, to any network or device. No question, the ability to work and play online using your smartphone is awfully convenient. But every single public access point you encounter is a chance for someone else to peek in and even steal sensitive information from you while you're online. And if your Wi-Fi is turned on, products like the WiFi Pineapple can trick your device into sharing information without your knowledge. To be safer when using your smartphone, laptop, or tablet, use only secured connections. Use a VPN connection, or just always skip free unsecured public Wi-Fi. Your phone still can use its own mobile data in plenty of places. It might cost a little more depending on your plan, but the added safety is often worth the money.

THE NATION-STATE THREAT No discussion of surveillance and mobile phones would be complete without a mention of Edward Snowden, who in 2013 stole a large number of files classified by the U.S. government as Secret, Top Secret, or higher. Regardless of whether you think he is a hero or traitor, he opened our eyes to the technical capabilities of well-funded actors, such as organized criminal gangs and nation-states.

In 2016, Snowden spoke on HBO about the issue, demonstrating how to remove components from a smartphone to remain completely safe (you can see this on YouTube). In VICE's documentary *State of Surveillance*, with Edward Snowden and Shane Smith, Snowden described why exactly you would want to remove the microphones and the cameras from your phone (note the plural tense of those components) and demonstrated just how to do it.

"Every part of private life today is on your phone," said Snowden. "They used to say that a man's home was his castle. Now, his phone is his castle."

Listening In Snowden was interested in IMSI-catchers, devices that, essentially, impersonate cell towers and intercept cell phones. Here's where we must warn that Snowden's understanding of how police use IMSI-catchers is absolutely flawed—use by U.S. police of IMSI-catchers is dramatically less common than Mr. Snowden believes. But he is correct in his assertion of the capability and ease of acquisition of an IMSI-catcher by police or private individuals for getting hold of the phone data you are sending. The solution is to follow security protocols appropriate for your risk profile, and follow them religiously.

Risk Assessment If you are an activist or protester or someone who takes on activists or

protesters, you should consider the likelihood of attacks against your electronic life to be rather high. If you're a soccer mom, you should consider the likelihood of a targeted attack rather low—that doesn't mean that you don't face mobile threats, such as malware, spyware, and the like. It just tells you how to set your expectations of privacy and therefore your security posture.

Staying Safe The Electronic Frontier Foundation (EFF) provides a very good starting place for this exercise in an article on its website titles "An Introduction to Threat Modeling." To give you an idea of how this works, we authors use encryption for our email and hard drives, and, wherever possible, we use encrypted voice and text through the application Signal. The EFF recommends Signal specifically because of the strength of its cryptographic implementation, its ease of use, and its "zero-knowledge" model— even if Signal itself is hacked, it cannot turn over any of your messages because it cannot read them. That's a powerful feature.

Finally, as we keep reminding you, encrypt your phone, and use a strong password to protect its contents—do not use a fingerprint. The reason for that is that U.S. courts have ruled it legal for police to use your fingerprints to unencrypt something, but it is currently not legal for the police to force you to turn over your password.

THE SPY IN YOUR POCKET We reached out to our friend, J.D. LeaSure, to ask what he thought of the cellular spying world. J.D. owns ComSec LLC, which is in the business of technical surveillance countermeasures—you know, in the movies when they have a guy come in and sweep for bugs? That's J.D.

"One of the worst culprits of cellular spying involves a program named FlexiSPY," he said. Highlights include call interception, SMS interception (including WhatsApp and other popular "secure" SMS applications), SMS tracking, password cracking, a digital recorder that can be set remotely not to ring/vibrate or light up, etc., etc. It's one bad mofo! Oh, and it works on both Android and iOS," says J.D.

"Another one is mSpy, which can track call logs, GPS location, and metadata about how the person is living his or her life—from calendar updates and text messages to email and web history. It, too, works with both Android and iOS.

"The best bug in the world is right there in your pocket . . . and adversaries know that your phone is never more than six feet away, and you always have it with you, and turned on."

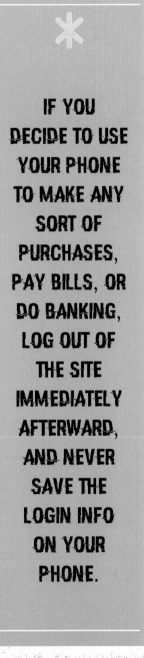

IF YOU DECIDE TO USE YOUR PHONE TO MAKE ANY SORT OF PURCHASES, PAY BILLS, OR DO BANKING, LOG OUT OF THE SITE IMMEDIATELY AFTERWARD, AND NEVER SAVE THE LOGIN INFO ON YOUR PHONE.

FINGERPRINT VERSUS PASSCODE In 2014, a test case made it to the Second Circuit Court in Virginia in *Commonwealth of Virginia v. David Charles Baust*. This is not a federal court but rather an important state court. Baust had been charged with trying to strangle his girlfriend. The state said that Baust and his girlfriend had set up video equipment in the bedroom, and the victim admitted that the video from that setup transmitted to and was saved on Baust's mobile phone (for exactly the reason you'd suspect). The state argued that the setup had captured the event on video, so it got a warrant for the phone. Baust refused to provide the fingerprint to unlock and decrypt the device, claiming that passcodes and fingerprints are protected by the Fifth Amendment, which prohibits forced self-incrimination. The state argued that the production of the credentials was not "testimonial," for the simple reason that it had already been established that the video was on the phone—the existence of the recording was a "foregone conclusion."

A Key Difference In his ruling, presiding judge Steven C. Frucci drew a very important distinction between using a passcode versus a fingerprint. It had been established in case law, the judge ruled, that a passcode represents testimonial communication. The ruling was determined because a passcode—unlike bodily measurements or fingerprints, or a voice exemplar or handwriting sample—is not a physical thing; instead, it is something that resides in a person's mind. Therefore, forcing the defendant to reveal his passcode would mean that the government is forcing him to testify and divulge potentially self-incriminating evidence.

On the other hand, the fingerprint is not considered testimony. Judge Frucci pointed to well-established concepts, stating that "There is a significant difference between the use of compulsion to extort communications from a defendant and compelling a person to engage in a conduct that may be incriminating. . . . The privilege offers no protection against compulsion to submit to fingerprinting, photography or measurements, to write

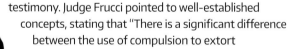

T/F

COPS HAVE A RIGHT TO TRACK YOUR PHONE

TRUE The case here is *United States v. Skinner.* The DEA tracked Mr. Skinner's vehicle by repeatedly "pinging" a phone it knew he had, as Skinner drove on public thoroughfares from New Mexico to Texas. When Skinner stopped for the night, the cops arrived and a drug-sniffing K-9 indicated the presence of drugs. Police searched; discovered the dope, the guns, and the phones; and Skinner and his son Samuel were arrested. In this case, the United States Court of Appeals for the Sixth Circuit ruled that "If a tool used to transport contraband gives off a signal that can be tracked for location, certainly the police can track the signal."

or speak for identification, to appear in court, to stand, to assume a stance, to walk, or to make a particular gesture."

A Legal Matter Basically, all that fancy legalese means that the court can't force you to produce the combination to a lock, but it can make you produce the key to a lock.

As a result of this ruling, it is considered a pretty solid bet in America that the government can make you produce your fingerprint, but it can't force you to produce your password or passcode. Lesson? Don't use fingerprints or other biometric identifiers like retinal scans or handprints to protect your data. Always use a strong passcode.

THE TAKEAWAY

You use your phone for just about everything in your life, so there's no one-size-fits-all set of security protocols. Think carefully and act accordingly.

BASIC SECURITY	• Use a good password—never your fingerprint. A good password is more than six characters or numbers, or a good pattern. • Encrypt your phone. • Use a phone-locator app in case it is stolen.
ADVANCED MEASURES	• Limit the number of days of email that can download to the phone. • Use a VPN for browsing in public. • Use 2FA for all apps that you possibly can. • Limit location services and Wi-Fi use. • Ensure limited metadata is saved with images.
TINFOIL-HAT BRIGADE	• All of the above—and remove the cameras and microphones from your smartphone. • Use encrypted DNS (will only fix Wi-Fi). • Regularly reflash your phone to factory settings. • Limit data usage.

TO KEEP YOUR PHONE TOTALLY SECURE WHEN NOT IN USE, TURN IT OFF COMPLETELY— AND THEN REMOVE THE BATTERY IF POSSIBLE TO AVOID ANY PASSIVE DATA COLLECTION.

GLOSSARY

Algorithm A process or set of rules to be followed in calculations or other problem-solving operations.

Botnet A network of computers liked together by malware.

Clickbait Something, such as a headline, designed to make readers want to click on a hyperlink, especially when the link leads to content of dubious value or interest.

Dossier A file containing detailed records on a particular person or subject.

Encryption The process of converting information or data into a code, especially to prevent unauthorized access.

Escrow Money or property held in trust by a third party to be turned over upon fulfillment of a condition.

Fraud Deceit or trickery.

Gambit A calculated move.

Hacking To gain illegal access to a computer network or system.

Impersonate To act as another person.

Incognito With one's identity concealed.

Infrastructure The basic physical and organizational structures needed for the operation of something.

Malware Software designed to interfere with a computer's normal functioning.

Parsimony The quality of being careful with money or resources.

Phishing A scam by which an Internet user is duped into revealing personal or confidential information which the scammer can use illicitly.

Precaution A measure taken beforehand to prevent harm.

Ransomware A type of malicious software designed to block access to a computer system until a sum of money is paid.

Reconnaissance A preliminary survey to gain information.

Scammer A person who conducts a fraudulent or deceptive act or operation.

Ubiquitous Being everywhere at the same time.

FOR FURTHER READING

Flores, Maria Antonieta. *The Language of Cybersecurity*. Laguna Hills: XML Press, 2018.

Kosseff, Jeff. *Cybersecurity Law*. Hoboken: Wiley, 2017.

Meeuwisse, Raef. *Cybersecurity for Beginners*. London, UK: Cyber Simplicity Ltd, 2017.

Meeuwisse, Raef. *Cybersecurity: Home and Small Business*. London, UK: Cyber Simplicity Ltd, 2016.

Singer, P.W., and Allan Friedman. *Cybersecurity and Cyberwar: What Everyone Needs to Know*. Oxford, UK: Oxford University Press, 2014.

FOR MORE INFORMATION

Be Ready, Be Informed

https://www.ready.gov/cybersecurity

Understand the fundamental concepts of cybersecurity and how to use them.

Homeland Security

https://www.dhs.gov/topic/cybersecurity

Learn about the cybersecurity strategies employed by the Department of Homeland Security.

Introduction to Cybersecurity

http://www.umuc.edu/academic-programs/cyber-security/about.cfm

Discover cybersecurity career opportunities and more.

What You Need to Know

https://www.forbes.com/sites/laurencebradford/2018/03/30/why-people-should-learn-about-cybersecurity-in-2018/#171136325d00

An informative article about how technology affects modern life.

INDEX

INDEX

N

NASA computers, hacking of, 19

Nickerson, Amanda, 42–43, 44

"Nigerian prince" scam, 36, 37

O

online presence, checking your, 44

online reputation, 45

P

Palin, Sarah, 19

parental control software, 56, 57

passwords, how to create and protect, 20–21

phishing

    defending yourself against, 18–19

    how to detect phishing emails, 18

    types of, 16, 17

    what it is, 16

R

red market, explanation of, 32

Riley v. California, 84

S

smartphone safety, 80–83

Snowden, Edward, 19, 88

Social Security numbers, 12, 13, 25, 27, 31

"Spanish prisoner" scam, 36–37

spearphishing, explanation of, 17

stalking/cyberstalking, 12, 42–43, 44, 55, 57, 63, 76

"Stranded in London" scam, 36

surveillance marketing, 74–75

Sutton, Willie, 29

T

tax return fraud, 12

trolls, 44–45

two-factor authentication, 21, 43

    2016 presidential election, hacking of, 19, 40

U

United States v. Skinner, 90

V

Valenti, Jessica, 44

vishing/smishing, explanation of, 17

voluntary disclosure of information, 16

W

West, Lindy, 45

whale phishing, explanation of, 17

white market, explanation of, 32

Wi-Fi, security of, 46–47

WikiLeaks, 19

Wozniak, Steve, 19

Y

Yastremskiy, Maksym "Maksik," 29

Z

Zuckerberg, Mark, 45